"If the owners of small and midsized companies read this book, it will totally change the way they look at workplace safety. It will transform their thinking about workplace safety from 'something you have to do for OSHA or the insurance company' to thinking of workplace safety as something that will make the company more efficient and more profitable. When business owners view workplace safety in this light, it allows them to manage their workers' compensation program as they would any other aspect of their business."

Mike Murrah, BCG Insurance Services,

"I have worked with both Steve Thompson and Dan Hopwood since 1991 and have found the two of them to be the best safety professionals in the business. Their knowledge of workplace safety issues and professionalism is of the highest caliber. I highly endorse their book and their principles."

Robert Stricker, Employment Law,
Law Offices of Stricker & Ball

"Steve and Dan's professional expertise comes through loud and clear. As I learned from them several years ago, good safety programs are always internally driven. Insurance brokers, agents and safety professionals can provide knowledge about ways to protect your workforce, but they can't instill a culture of safety."

Bill Litjen, President, G.S. Levine Insurance Services

"Being in the health care field I have found that chronic pain issues are often associated with the workplace. It is imperative for companies to take the appropriate measures to help mitigate the potential risks. Steve and Dan have done a great job in showing them the way."

Aaron Brooks, President, Perfect Postures, Inc.

"Health and safety on the job should be a priority for every company, not just those with multi-million dollar budgets. Steve and Dan make this information accessible to every business large and small. They take it a step further to help the reader see that workplace safety is a "people" issue and not a 'numbers' issue. As an owner of a small business, I found this book clear, concise and user friendly."

Anthony B. Carey M.A., CSCS, CES, CEO Function First
[Author of *The Pain-Free Program: A Proven Method to Relieve Back, Neck, Shoulder and Joint Pain*]

"*Workplace Safety* is an excellent resource. This book should be read by all business owners who genuinely want to take care of their employees, control injuries and manage their workers' compensation costs."

Chris Liechty, CSP, ARM, Safety Consultant

"This book offers a simple approach to the development of a health and safety program. It is easy to follow and the content is valuable for both the inexperienced and seasoned professional. It is a good resource to add to your safety library."

Michelle Eisenberg MPH PT,
President, Ergonomic Evaluation & Training

Workplace Safety

A Guide for Small and Midsized Companies

DAN HOPWOOD
AND
STEVE THOMPSON

John Wiley & Sons, Inc.

For general information on our other products and services, or technical support, please
contact our Customer Care Department within the United States at 800-762-2974, outside
the United States at 317-572-3993 or fax 317-572-4002.

Wiley also publishes its books in a variety of electronic formats. Some content that appears in
print may not be available in electronic books.

For more information about Wiley products, visit our Web site at *www.wiley.com*.

Library of Congress Cataloging-in-Publication Data:
Thompson, Steve, 1960 Oct. 27–
    Workplace safety : a guide for small and midsized companies / Stephen Thompson, Dan
Hopwood.
        p. cm.
    Includes index.
    ISBN-13: 978-0-7821-3604-3 (cloth)
    ISBN-10: 0-7821-3604-4 (cloth)
    1. Industrial safety—United States—Handbooks, manuals, etc. 2. Small business—United
States—Safety measures—Handbooks, manuals, etc. I. Hopwood, Dan. II. Title.
T55.T48 2006
658.3'82—dc22
                                                                                2006005663

Printed in the United States of America
10   9   8   7   6   5   4   3   2   1

Contents

Preface

The practice of workplace safety has seen incredible advances in the last 30 years. It's not that there were few in the decades prior to the early 1970s, it's that the speed of the advancements has quickened. Many of the advancements are technologically based, while others fall within the regulatory realm. Still others have been found in how best to train employees and motivate them to be as safe as possible.

Without question, though, considerable workplace safety challenges remain. These challenges take the form of injuries and illnesses, economic sanctions as a result of regulatory citations, and financial loss due to the many uninsured consequences a company faces when exposed to personnel injuries and illnesses. Without business owners and management leading the safety charge, undertaking specific safety and health measures and the recognition that employees need to be involved in the workplace safety processes at all times, the challenges will not abate.

This book is about attacking those challenges in ways that are not complicated but can easily be embedded in your current business management activities. To that end, this book is designed for the management team of the small and/or midsize business. We recognize that the terms "small" and "midsized" may have different meanings to our readers. However, we are talking about companies that have very flat management hierarchy and that divvy up the safety and risk management tasks among multiple supervisors and employees. Such organizations generally may not have the resources for a full time safety professional or someone dedicated to safety. This book is for you, that multitasking manager or business owner, because there is a way to handle workplace safety without it being a burden. There are ways to handle safety without having an advanced safety education, and there are ways to ensure your company builds safety into its core values, mission, and goals. This book will help define that path and show you the way.

Our workplace safety focus is one that applies to all management, not just those with special skills, degrees, or certifications. Without question, educational experiences in the sciences, business, or human resources management and psychology would all be helpful, but none is a prerequisite. We have not written a book that is highly technical. In fact, we have purposely avoided that. Why? For many people, the technical challenges may block initiative and progress. Our job is to get you started, not slow you down.

We'll help you get started in several ways. These include discussing the background of workplace safety, why it's important, and what the core competencies are to being successful. When you finish reading this book, you'll understand the relationship of injuries and illnesses to regulatory mandates, financial management, as well as your short- and long-term business goals. In addition, you'll be able to perform a baseline assessment and, through critical questioning, implement those best practices which should be included in your efforts.

This book answers the question of what workplace safety is for you. It goes on to guide you through needs assessment, highlights training requirements, and provides methodologies and examples of how to write and focus your safety plans. We also felt it very important to provide a few examples of specific safety and health considerations—hazards, if you will—and discuss their controls. This is very important to the process of recognizing that not every business is the same and that there is no single, unified plan that works for everyone. You will need to develop a workplace safety program that is directly related to your operations, the exposures that exist, and the controls necessary to reduce injuries and illnesses.

We end the book with a review of several advanced topics, including emergency response and business continuity planning. We also highlight the basics of risk management and how they can be integrated into your planning efforts. In addition, our discussion of morals and ethics is extremely apropos in today's business world. Our review of workers' compensation is designed to provide one link from workplace safety to managing the financial impact of injuries and illnesses. No better example exists than workers' compensation.

The "greatest lessons learned" is our final salvo. Feedback from some top safety and health professionals and the lessons they have learned over the past few years will be enlightening and serve as a source of motivation to you—to start your safety efforts or to enhance them as might be needed.

We recognize we cover a lot of ground in this book. We also know that if you get started, you will accomplish many positive things and your workplace safety program and efforts will continue to improve. You'll know if you're headed in the right direction by looking at the best practices questions in the Selected References and Resources section of the book and online at www.workplacesafety.com. The more you can answer affirmatively, the more you have accomplished and the closer you are to developing a winning safety program. Those you answer "no" or "maybe" point directly to where your program efforts need work. We are also confident that reviewing the best practices questions regularly will serve you well.

As practicing safety professionals, teachers, and business managers, we have learned many safety lessons over our combined nearly 50 years of experience. Foremost among them is that to achieve any workplace safety successes, a first step has to be taken. Whether an audit or best practices review, a foundation must be constructed and plans drafted. The more your safety efforts truly relate to what your employees do and the specific hazards they face, the better outcomes you will experience. We also have learned that safety efforts are never a straight line; they are rather, a journey whose starting point you will visit more than once.

We're confident with some effort, teamwork and critical thinking, your journey will be successful. In fact, you'll likely enjoy it.

Dan Hopwood and Steve Thompson
San Diego, California
August 2006

Acknowledgements

We want to thank our family, friends, and colleagues for your encouragement, collaboration, and contributions to this book. We also owe a debt of gratitude to Sheck Cho and his team at Wiley for their direction, guidance, support, and trust in us.

DAN HOPWOOD

To Leslie, for supporting me in all of my journeys, and for staying my number 1; to Kylie and Kendall, the most beautiful, talented and thoughtful daughters a dad could wish for.

To Steve Thompson, no finer a person and professional could this task have been undertaken with.

To my big sister Jan, the defender of all I do; Bob, Charlene and Dennis Anderson for sheltering me from the storm and to Dick and Anita—I know life would be incredibly different without all of you having been part of mine.

To Drs. James Noto and Tee Guidotti, who mentored when I needed a mentor and led when I needed leading.

To Bill Carolan and Greg Cybulski—the world needs more like you two to count on and to Mark Evans whose support and friendship has been immeasurable in many ways.

STEVE THOMPSON

Joann Thompson—wife, friend, and support throughout the journey.

Thompson, Wante, Tirotta, McKeever, brother, sister, and all "related" families throughout the US—I'm fortunate to have such wonderfully supportive and caring relatives.

Roy Thompson—at a young age teaching me that all people are equal and that it's important to do the job right.

Lorraine Thompson—for teaching me that living simply is OK, and that volunteering is good for the soul.

Ray Hunter—you taught me to always put the customer first, and to never stop "giving back."

Branden Thompson—my son, you have changed me through your creative soul and spirit. I am honored to be in your life.

Brian Harris—my best friend and confidant. You never judge me even when I've headed down the wrong path—you have always been there for me.

Camille Currier—the most resilient and courageous business partner and friend anyone could ever hope for.

Dan Hopwood—teacher, boss, and now author and business partner. You're the finest safety professional in the business, and I consider myself extremely fortunate working beside you all of these years. Without you my friend, there wouldn't be a book!

Cait Casey—the most passionate safety professional anywhere. Thank you Cait for always steering me in the direction of "doing what's right for the working guy."

Cathi Marx—for teaching me the importance of really listening to every word a person speaks. You inspire me to be the best I can be.

Scott Primiano and Richard Coskren—colleagues, mentors, and leadership guides. Thank you for believing in me, and making me a part of your team.

G.S. Levine Insurance family—for being my first customer and the foundation on which we have built our business. Thank you Gary, Bill, Jeff, and Ross.

Phyllis Simmons—without you, this book would not have been written. Thank you for thinking of me.

Allison Fowler—for your safety enthusiasm and passion. I'm always inspired by your energy.

Elise Fischer—the most creative, innovative safety leader on the planet.

Chris Liechty—for teaching me to always be objective and never judge.

Craig Larson and Mon Uson—for always trusting in me and allowing me to experiment.

SDSU Safety Students—Eric, Julie, Mary, Wally, David, Lance, Al, Bob, Russ, Angela, and so many others. You are all stellar representatives in our field of work.

Kate Montgomery—for always being so passionate about taking care of people and "fighting against" injustice.

Mike Murrah—friend, supporter, and business partner. You taught me the importance of using the word "injured worker" and everything important about "the industry."

Rick Sanchez—for showing me (through your actions) the importance of "balance."

Michelle Eisenberg—my friend and ergonomics mentor and guide— you are the best in your field.

Gene Magré—innovator and entrepreneur—for encouraging me to start my own business; then trusting me to help you in yours.

CHAPTER 1

Introduction: What Is Workplace Safety?

Hundreds of books have been written on the broad field of safety and health management, and thousands more can be added when considering specific safety and health considerations and processes focused on given industries. Coupled with academic research, journal articles, and regulatory writings, the field of workplace safety has a considerable volume of work behind it. In large part, these materials have been published for the safety practitioner or those with some existing knowledge of workplace safety and some academic background or training. Such books, guides, articles, and research papers have created a bridge from the basics of safety and health, to program development and management, to more complex issues, such as specific hazard controls, toxicology, and the role human behavior plays in managing workplace safety, with toxicology and human behavior serving as general examples. In addition, many provide information and guidance toward regulatory compliance. All were written with the goal of reducing the potential for workers and an organization's other constituents, such as the general public, to become injured or ill. In most cases, these writings have focused on a specific readership; a few have been much broader in their scope, hoping to appeal to wide audiences. Very few have recognized the distinction in the size of a business or, more specifically, the differences in available managerial and economic resources as well as the technical capabilities within a company or those assigned to manage workplace safety.

Clearly, then, the ability to manage workplace safety effectively hinges on several critical considerations, such as:

- Establishing a clear commitment to safety
- Identifying unsafe actions and conditions
- Providing resources for safety training (including advanced safety training for a supervisor)
- Assigning someone the task of safety or assuming it yourself, and providing the resources (time and money)

Who should read this book? Although many will benefit from a review of its contents, this book's major audiences are intended to be the executive of a small-to-midsized company tasked with workplace safety (among many other duties!), the human resources professional, the operations manager, or those vested with collateral safety and health management duties, along with individuals relatively new to the field of workplace safety management.

There are several ways to answer the opening question of this book, "What is workplace safety?" and its sister question, "Why is workplace safety important?" We'll begin with some thoughts on the challenges of managing such programs as a mechanism to begin addressing the query. Although seemingly easy, the answer focuses upon several critical considerations that are equally important; for example, it's just as critical to discuss the challenges of managing workplace safety programs as it is to highlight the objective steps that actually guide a workplace safety program to fruition. Both of these considerations are no more important than the development of the skills to identify hazards in the workplace or the ability to maintain effective workplace safety training programs. As you will see, workplace safety management is a complex set of activities, all focused on one outcome: reducing or eliminating injuries, illnesses, and incidents.

This chapter discusses additional considerations focused on managing programs, understanding the link between knowledge of operations and workplace safety, identifying hazards, and getting programs started. We also outline some of the major challenges those responsible for workplace safety (you) will face on the journey to successful program development and deployment.

For many, the management of workplace safety programs has long been seen as a complicated issue. This perspective exists for many reasons. Such reasons are found in the confidence necessary to:

- Deploy a workplace safety program
- Truly understand the nature of the hazards your business and workers are exposed to
- Ensure that regulatory mandates are being met

Each is an essential goal within a workplace safety program, and separately they comprise critical aspects of the program. Taken together, they begin to set the stage for success; however, the safety practitioner is faced with many other challenges in developing an effective workplace safety program and ensuring its success. This chapter, as it answers the question "What is workplace safety management?" also addresses the management issues noted above and more importantly, why it is important to assure their success.

To a large extent, this book is designed to moderate those challenges by breaking workplace safety management into discrete, bite-size elements, both *tactical* and *strategic*. Additionally, this book is intended to assist the reader to capitalize on the efforts required to manage workplace safety programs while tasked with a myriad of other responsibilities. Workplace safety management must be given its proper place within an organization's many initiatives, and this can be accomplished only by achieving both an understanding of need and the basic skills to build a program and control it effectively.

Workplace safety programs are only one among many for which time and other resources must be made available. These programs must receive the proper attention, but neither more or less than necessary. It is best, however, to blend workplace safety management programs with operations and other programs. In larger organizations, these programs may be managed by human resources, for example. However, in the small and midsized company, management most often falls to you.

By understanding the strategic and tactical aspects of workplace safety management programs, and their related elements, you as "safety practitioner" can dedicate your time and that of others, and rally the necessary resources to ensure that a meaningful program is constructed. Without this understanding, something critical will be missing from the final product.

There is one very important distinction to point out now. This book is about the management of a workplace safety program. Our intention is to provide you with the insights necessary to structure and manage a program; we do not aim to teach you each and every intricacy of being a safety professional.

WORKPLACE SAFETY MANAGEMENT IS STRATEGIC AND TACTICAL

As you move through the chapters in this book, a picture will be painted, if you will, with the broad strokes of the strategic and tactical aspects of workplace safety programs (see Exhibit 1.1). The detail will be painted as the book unfolds. These efforts include highlighting the attributes of workplace safety programs and the activities necessary to ensure their success.

The strategic aspects include the rationale for:

- Programs
- Management commitment and support
- Regulatory compliance
- Program development and deployment

EXHIBIT 1.1   STRATEGIC AND TACTICAL ASPECTS OF HEALTH AND SAFETY MANAGEMENT

Strategic Aspects	Tactical Aspects
Rationale for programs	Hazard identification
Management commitment	Hazard control
Regulatory compliance	Links to other human resources programs
Program development and deployment	Incident investigations Training

As you might suspect, the strategic aspects of workplace safety management plans lay the foundation for planning efforts and are those intended to ensure that plans are not short-lived.

In addition, the picture will include the tactical elements of workplace safety management. These elements include:

- Hazard identification
- Hazard control
- Linkages to other management functions (i.e., disciplinary measures and access to employee assistance programs; see Exhibit 1.2)
- Investigation of incidents, such as injuries, illnesses, and near misses
- Employee health and safety training

Understanding the links to programs associated with workplace safety, or those that mutually benefit safety, are important for a number of very good reasons, including:

- If there are other programs that benefit from workplace safety activities and programs, management tends to lend a greater deal of support. This is the case for many reasons, including program-related economies of scale (i.e., through the development of one program, another benefits). Such is the case with workplace safety management and workers' compensation programs, for example.
- Cost control. As you might suspect, controlling injuries and illnesses also helps an organization control and even reduce its workers' compensation insurance costs.
- Greater degree of centralized management and program control.

EXHIBIT 1.2   RELATED HUMAN RESOURCES
                 PROGRAM EXAMPLES

Employee assistance

Benefits

Discipline

Americans with Disabilities Act

Early return to work

These are particularly important for the small and midsized company, where it is typical for members of the management team to wear more than one hat and have responsibility for more than one function.

More detail will be provided on both the strategic and tactical aspects of workplace safety management in other chapters.

The tactical aspects of safety and health programs are the "what" of programs, compared to the strategic aspects, which are the "why." One cannot succeed without the other, and as you can see from Exhibit 1.2, many other human resources functions are related to workplace safety or are aided by workplace safety efforts.

So far we have been setting the stage for *what workplace safety is.* It should be fairly clear that such programs are not comprised entirely of just written words. If they were, then every company would borrow someone else's and declare it is finished with the planning process. The authors, with nearly 50 combined years of experience, can tell you that is never the case.

WORKPLACE PROGRAMS: MANAGEMENT AT ITS BEST

Workplace safety management—and *management* is a key operative word in our overview—is the synthesis of three very important considerations:

Consistent management effort

Employee involvement

Programming and the practice of the tactical aspects of workplace safety management

Consistent Management Effort

Even though many employers have tried, it is rare for a workplace safety program to succeed without consistent management effort (putting a plan together), involvement (leading by example), and dedicating the proper resources (time, materials, and money) to a program. There is a wide variation in what may be required from the resource allocation perspective among organizations. This is a function of size, the nature of the hazards employees are exposed to, regulatory requirements, and many other factors.

Employee Involvement

As we have uncovered during the development and analysis of literally hundreds of workplace safety programs, without the proverbial employee buy-in, few programs have any chance for success. This is the case for many reasons. Key among them is that employees feel a keen desire to be part of meaningful activities, and in fact, most often they have a considerable amount to contribute to the planning process. Who, for example, knows how to conduct operations better than your experienced employees? They may very well have recommendations or enhancements to safety procedures that can make great differences in reducing future hazards and employee exposure to injury or illness. Later chapters will cover this in more detail.

Practicing the Tactical Aspects

Workplace safety programs should be used as tools to improve operations and processes. This cannot happen if the tactical aspects of programs are not consistently utilized or practiced.

For example, organizations that enforce the tactical element of incident investigations are able to determine if an unsafe act or unsafe condition was the underlying cause of an injury or illness. With this information, employee training can be improved, or better focused, and operational improvements can be implemented.

The definition of *management* includes planning, leading, organizing, and controlling. There is no better way to frame the functional aspects of workplace safety management. Workplace safety management programs perform poorly when they are reactive in nature. As you will learn soon, to be reactive implies that the hazards associated with a job or tasks are allowed to exist before any preventive action is taken. The implication is that only outcomes (injuries and illnesses) are responded to. Thus, the reactive approach never attacks the root causes of these outcomes. Many employers respond only to that which has already happened and never look at what is causing an injury or illness to develop. Clearly, this approach is contraindicated if a management program that works is in existence.

A program that has plan-ahead features, such as hazard inspections and more detailed job hazard analyses, is capable of identifying physical, chemical, biological, and ergonomic as well as psychological and operational hazards and of mitigating them prior to adverse outcomes. As you might suspect, the ability to identify and mitigate these hazards is the hallmark of better-than-average workplace safety plans.

Workplace safety management does include *planning*—planning for resources (whether people or materials) and all of the activities that go along with maintaining a management program. Once marshaled, these resources, particularly the organization's human resources, require utilization. All human resources must be "playing from the same page and sheet of music" regarding workplace safety management. If this is not the case, then a discordant program effort will follow, with the result being injuries and illnesses.

The *leadership* associated with workplace safety programs actually can come from several sources. However, it is absolutely essential that a great deal of program leadership be vested with the individual or individuals who actually oversee the program and are held accountable for its results. To put it simply, those who are the consumers of the program—the employees—require a very clear picture of who's in charge.

Because workplace safety programs require resources, they must be *organized* to obtain peak efficiencies. The first three management elements typically are linked to the strategic aspects of a workplace safety program. The tactical aspects traditionally are tied to the management element of *control*. This link is fairly simple, since the tactical aspects of workplace safety plans include training, incident investigations, hazard identification, and hazard control.

Workplace safety management requires program planning and resource availability. It also requires active leadership and organization to assure consistent deployment. In addition, workplace safety management requires controlling exposures to injury and illness. This criterion further delineates what workplace safety management is: those tactics that are implemented to reduce and, whenever possible, eliminate the factors that allow injuries and illnesses to develop. These factors are found in both unsafe acts and unsafe conditions.

Workplace safety management programs are not self-written or self-sustaining. As with many other programs, as they are integrated within the fabric of an organization and nurtured, it is much easier to maintain them and ensure that they are having a meaningful impact.

UNDERSTANDING TWO BASIC DEFINITIONS

Workplace safety management requires an understanding of two basic definitions. More specifically, it requires defining the *differences* in health and safety. Understanding health and safety—the words and what they mean—is essential to your success in managing such programs. We want to take a different approach with the definitions of health and safety. Sure, we could grab a dictionary and look up what it has to say about the two words. Those are textbook definitions. Although they are important and certainly help to establish a framework for our understanding of program needs, we want you to become familiar with the working world definitions. Familiarity will make all the difference when you begin to apply the tactical aspects of workplace safety management programs on a consistent basis.

HEALTH AND SAFETY = ILLNESSES AND INJURIES

First, we will review workplace safety from their individual attributes and central tendencies. We mention tendencies because what we are going to share *is not an absolute* but a very good guide and will make your management of programs easier and the focus of your planning efforts much more clear. It is absolutely essential to differentiate health and safety in your program efforts. Why?

The recognition of hazards and their control is directly related to the harm they may cause if a worker is exposed to a particular hazard. For example, if we are concerned about an employee's exposure to an organic vapor, it is essential not only to know what substance is in use, but how to measure for the presence of its vapors. It is equally important to be able to recognize the signs and symptoms of exposure or overexposure. Exposures to organic vapors generally result in illnesses, not injuries. For example, overexposure to the chemical degreaser 1,1,1 trichloroethane can result in nervous system (neuropathies) and visual (oculomotor) abnormalities and, with exposure or contact, may result in respiratory distress or dermatitis due to drying out the skin. Neuropathies and oculomotor disorders are *illnesses,* while respiratory distress generally is and dermatitis is an *injury.*

What's more important is that the general tendency (again, not an absolute!) is for illnesses that develop to have done so from chronic exposures. Although some illnesses have rapid onsets, most occur over time—hours, days, or longer, but rarely immediate; again, this is referred to as chronic exposure.

The relationship is this (see Exhibit 1.3): Adverse health effects tend to occur over time (they are chronic) and tend to result in illnesses. Injuries, however, tend to be acute (i.e., they happen very suddenly).

The flip side to our health analogy is that injuries occur most often from employees' exposure to conditions that result in a traumatic, quick event—an event that is acute. An example that we can all relate to is the amputation of a finger in a table saw or a worker with a foreign object in the eye as a result of grinding metal without proper personal protective equipment. In the first case, the loss of the finger is immediate, not something that develops over time. In the second case, the foreign object at the least will result in eye irritation and at the worst can result in the loss of vision.

The importance of distinguishing injury-producing situations from those that result in illnesses is rooted in both hazard identification and hazard control.

Many employers are guilty of attempting a unified methodology toward the resolution of injuries and illnesses. Unfortunately, no such single methodology exists, with perhaps the exception of total avoidance of hazards. Although no one would get hurt or become ill from this approach, there would also be no production; thus it is not a practical approach. One of the more common unified approaches to resolving injuries and illnesses, for example, is to recommend "more" training.

| EXHIBIT 1.3 | DIFFERENTIATING THE TENDENCIES IN INJURIES AND ILLNESSES |

	Health or Safety Focus	Tendency Is to Be:
Injuries	Safety	Acute
Illnesses	Health	Chronic

Even though workplace safety training is essential, it is not the end all. In fact, we have used this quote in management seminars and speeches over the years:

You cannot train away the woes of the world.

What does this quote mean? Let's use a hypothetical scenario to make a point.

As a safety practitioner, you either know or have been advised that there have been several back injuries in the shipping and receiving department. You go to the department, meet with the supervisor, and ask a few questions about the injuries. You determine that some have occurred with newer employees while others among experienced staff. After the review, it is your recommendation that all shipping and receiving employees be provided additional lifting and material handling training.

Once the training has been provided, you begin keeping a closer eye on the development of injuries. You find that not only have they continued, but the frequency has actually increased! Puzzled? You shouldn't be.

As a *unified* approach to injury resolution, training has some distinct drawbacks, in spite of many benefits. Training does not change the size or the shape of the materials being lifted and moved. Training does not reduce the weight of the objects being lifted, nor does it modify the frequency of the lifts performed by the shipping and receiving employees. Training does nothing to alter the height of the shelving boxes are placed on or the length of the walk necessary once a box has been lifted. You see, even if you train an employee how to lift safely, there remain many task hazards that require mitigation to reduce the exposure to injury fundamentally.

Training is quick and generally cost-effective (with the exception, from a safety standpoint, of those areas where there is high employee turnover). Training *does not,* however, change the fundamental nature of a process, task, material, or machine to cause harm. Training is an adjunct to other sound safety activities. In the last example, training can supplement reducing the weight of boxes being lifted, how far they must be carried, and how often they are lifted. The underlying rationale is that to truly control injury- and illness-producing situations, appropriate physical (also referred to as *engineering controls*) and/or administrative controls must be implemented, not just along with training but also before training. Implementing these controls requires that you understand if a hazard is going to (likely) result in an injury or illness.

The last sentence may seem self-evident. However, if the likelihood of injury or illness development and their distinction can be determined, then three things are possible:

Appropriate preinjury or illness physical controls and mitigation activities can be implemented.

Required personal protective equipment can be obtained and its use enforced, and other administrative controls can be implemented.

Training can be provided that supplements injury and illness control activities and teaches and further validates the importance of employees knowing how to utilize required safeguards and personal protective equipment and the appropriate steps to perform a task.

In many ways, it is easier to correct the factors that result in injuries and illnesses after they have manifested. If we can establish a cause-and-effect relationship, we should be able to resolve much of the hazard potential prior to employees becoming injured or ill. This approach is critical and one that should be repeated, almost like a mantra. Control or reduce the hazards, and you both lessen the reliance on training and manage the adverse outcomes (injuries and illnesses).

We want to highlight the fact that injuries and illnesses do not normally come from the same hazards (although some do, such as the physical injuries associated with repetitive tasks and the psychological stress related to such tasks). Thus, hazard-specific controls must be adopted. If you were unable, for instance, to determine if the injuries in the last example arose from physical hazards versus chemical hazards, then improper controls almost certainly would be initiated. At the very least, the potential for injuries would remain unchanged; in fact, it might actually worsen. Taking the time to distinguish the type of hazard that exists will better your mitigation strategies and ultimately reduce injuries and illnesses. We discuss these thoughts more in chapters that follow.

WORKPLACE SAFETY PROGRAMS: THEIR PURPOSE

Chapter 2 focuses on the elements of programs that must exist and some methodologies for assessing their existence and strength. However, it is important to highlight here, albeit briefly, the overarching purposes of workplace safety programs.

It has been shown time and time again that safe companies are productive companies and almost always show a greater return on their monetary and personnel investments. Turnover is lower—that's another positive correlation. Further, companies that make every effort to enforce safe working protocols almost always find themselves in compliance with regulatory mandates, such as those associated with federal or state OSHA (Occupational Health and Safety Administration) regulations, and reduce the potential for citations and economic sanctions from these regulatory agencies.

From a big-picture perspective, there exist several general reasons to maintain workplace safety programs. These include but are by no means are limited to:

- Employee retention is frequently improved.
- Productivity is generally better than average.
- Regulatory compliance efforts are enhanced.
- Economic sanctions are potentially reduced.
- Hazards are mitigated, reducing injuries and illnesses.
- Related programs and the link to health and safety, such as those found in Exhibit 1.2, are improved.
- Process improvements are commonly identified.

For many of us who are responsible for safety and health programs on a regular basis, our purpose is fairly simple: Provide a long-term plan that is successful in protecting people from injury, illness, and death, in complying with regulations, and in controlling the associated financial costs with loss. Many organizations, however, require deeper understanding and validation. For those, the preceding list should be helpful. And, of course, we hope those who need additional urging will study this entire book.

WHO'S RESPONSIBLE FOR WORKPLACE SAFETY PROGRAMS?

There's an old adage in the workplace safety arena that everyone is responsible for workplace safety, and that adage is true enough. We know, however, that not only does someone within an organization need to take on the responsibility for the development, deployment, and maintenance of workplace safety programs, that person also needs to be held accountable for its performance. Do not let the issue of accountability frighten you from jumping right in and taking on the critical tasks associated with such plans. Our experience is that making an honest effort and focusing on the known injury- and illness-producing activities first will serve you in good stead. That is, you will be hedging your bets toward success.

Our review highlights the areas of responsibility that we have noted to be historically effective. To that end, it is helpful to consider the issue of responsibility like a system, if you will. Systems require the interaction of several components to operate effectively. Remove or damage one of the components, and the system either fails or works at something less than optimal capacity.

A "responsibility system," then, is comprised of employees, supervision, management team members, and senior management, including those in ownership positions. Looking at responsibility as a system should provide many readers with some degree of comfort. Why?

Managing workplace safety programs does not have to be done alone or in a vacuum; reaching out and utilizing various personnel from your organization is an excellent tactic. For example, many employees, especially those with experience, do a fine job in identifying hazards. They have experienced the stresses of a particular job and may have seen coworkers injured doing many of the same tasks that they perform. Thus, although this is not universally true, employees are excellent additions to the safety team, serving as hazard identifiers. One practical example of this approach is the utilization of employees on inspection teams just prior to conducting a safety committee meeting.

Employees

Think of safety responsibility almost like a hierarchical organizational chart. At the base of this chart are employees; they have responsibility for complying with all workplace safety rules and regulations of your company. In addition, all employees should be vested with the responsibilities associated with hazard identification, especially those employees who occupy a spot on safety committees or other company committees related to workplace safety. This becomes increasingly important as the range of control of any given supervisor or manager expands. More important, this responsibility actively engages employees in the workplace safety program. Many organizations choose to formally recognize employee contributions in this regard.

A timeless benefit of employee involvement and responsibility for safety-related functions as opposed to just outcomes (e.g., not getting injured) is that you are planting the seeds of safety in your supervisors-in-training or the next "safety director." In addition, based on their skills and knowledge of safety procedures, some employees make sound additions to your training team. By selecting employees carefully, you can easily spread the footprint of safety throughout an organization.

Provide responsibility, with appropriate training and recognition, and employees will almost always reward you for your faith in their capabilities.

Supervisors

As you move up the hierarchy, supervisors need not only to comply with established company policy, they must lead by example. They also will have some responsibilities toward ensuring that their teams are following the same policies and assisting with training, and they are a critical asset in identifying hazards that lead to injuries and illnesses. More important, since supervisors are normally at the point of attack—that is, they are supervising personnel who are actually conducting the tasks within a company—they are often best suited to implementing day-to-day safety improvements. The controls supervisors are able to implement may be the most important safety responsibility they possess. Such controls might include retraining an employee, replacing a guard on a machine, or enforcing company policy and referring an employee for disciplinary action.

Many organizations hold supervisory personnel responsible for workplace safety activities and further reward or penalize them at performance review intervals. Such an approach is beneficial as it assists in perpetuating the activities that lead to safe working behaviors. Please note that we said "perpetuating the activities," not recognizing "outcomes." Rewarding outcomes (the frequency or severity of work-related injuries or illnesses) can have drawbacks (i.e., stimulating underreporting of injuries, near misses, or hazards in general), while recognizing the activities surrounding workplace safety has next to no drawbacks.

Management Team

The management team, generally a smaller subset of the organization and higher still on the hierarchical structure, has the responsibility of confirming that hazard mitigation activities have taken place and that supervisors are meeting their responsibilities. Further, it is usual for a member of the management team, if not specifically dedicated, to be known as or referred to as the safety manager. The responsibilities of a safety manager span both the strategic and the tactical elements of workplace safety reviewed earlier in this chapter. To a large extent, the responsibilities of members of the management team, especially the person occupying the predominant role, are outlined in Chapter 2.

Safety managers and other management team members obtain and assign safety-related resources, write plans, conduct or assist with training, review incidents, and implement agreed-on recommendations designed to reduce the exposure to the injury- or illness-producing acts or conditions.

Many people believe that management is where the "safety rubber meets the road." Breakdowns at this level in regard to safety responsibilities almost universally result in a degradation of workplace safety programs and their performance.

Senior Management and Ownership

At the peak of the hierarchical structure is senior management and/or ownership. Just a few of senior management's responsibilities are assigning management tasks, ensuring they are completed with a purpose that is focused on achieving safe working conditions and reducing injuries and illnesses, and serving as the biggest safety cheerleader in the organization.

You are ultimately responsible for workplace safety program deployment, approval of expenditures to ensure safety and safeguards are being deployed, and validating regulatory compliance. These all fall within the purview of senior management. Without support or through benign neglect, you can easily put the brakes on meaningful safety activities. The time for safety, the energy that is required, as well as the resources, all flow from the support, participation, and involvement of senior managers or owners.

To sum up this section: Everyone has a role and many responsibilities when it comes to workplace safety.

KEY CONCEPTS: THE TWO MOST CRITICAL ONES

It is imperative that you recognize that the events that lead to workplace injuries and illness emanate from only one of two situations: *unsafe acts* and *unsafe conditions.* If you can remember these two fundamental reasons why people are hurt or become ill at work, you will do a much better job of building your workplace safety program and, perhaps more important, determining the safety controls requiring implementation to manage exposure to unsafe acts or conditions.

To put it simply, by controlling, reducing, or eliminating unsafe acts and conditions, injuries and illness will be reduced as well. Most publications indicate that 80 percent or more of workplace injuries and illnesses are the result of unsafe acts. This statistic tends to indicate that someone—an employee or supervisor performing a task, for example—performs an unsafe act, such as using a saw without its guard, driving without seat belts, or typing for extended periods of time without taking breaks to reduce the potential for a repetitive motion injury. We understand that in the small and midsize company, you or those in a supervisory role may perform day-to-day tasks. Thus, it's important to understand that front-line employees are not the only ones responsible for unsafe actions; supervisors and management may be equally at fault.

Unsafe conditions (trip-and-fall hazards, chemicals left out in open containers, a vehicle with poor brakes, etc.) that are left unchecked comprise the remainder of workplace-related injuries and illnesses. For many reasons, regulations among them, today's working conditions are vastly improved over those of 5 to 10 years ago, and certainly over those of 15 to 20 years ago. Although conditions that result in injuries and illness still exist, and will continue to do so, tremendous improvements have been made.

We want you to remember the distinctions between unsafe acts and conditions. Correcting unsafe acts and conditions frequently requires different and often very specific approaches. The recommendations you make to reduce employee exposure to unsafe acts and conditions will be repaid several times over. In addition, by knowing the differences between unsafe acts and conditions, your recommendations for safety improvement will be much more specific and thus have a greater potential for success.

CHALLENGES FOR THOSE PRACTICING SAFETY

This text aims to assist you in facing a variety of challenges. The discussion that follows sets the tone for the remainder of the book and, perhaps, for additional and more advanced study on your part. Recognizing the challenges and preparing for them will also serve to better prepare you for tasks you face in workplace safety management activities within your organization.

As a safety practitioner, you will face many challenges. Our brief discussion is limited to the four challenges we think you need to prepare for most (and this book will help overcome) as you look at enhancing the health and safety of where you work.

Challenge 1: Understanding Operations

No one knows your business better than you. A common challenge exists when companies assign workplace safety responsibilities to those unfamiliar with your operations. To the extent that they do not know how your company manufactures its products, how items are transported, where raw materials come from and how they are processed, for example, workplace safety efforts will be hampered. How can a workplace safety program be effective if operations are not understood? Or, further, how can resolutions to workplace hazards be recommended?

If you assign someone the task of creating your workplace safety program, that person must get out among the staff and experience what they do for a living. They must hear the sounds; feel the heat, so to speak, and other sensations, such as vibrations; look at the equipment that is used; and get a clear picture of their duties. Armed with this information, this person will author a better program, conduct better training, and do a much better job of investigating injuries. These considerations are from both a strategic and tactical perspective (see Exhibit 1.1.)

Challenge 2: Understanding the Nature of Hazards

Although we spend considerably more time on this issue in Chapter 2, when we discuss hazard assessments, you need to be aware that one of your challenges rests with truly understanding the hazards that your employees are exposed to. Of course, this challenge is directly related to the first one:

If you understand operations, you will be able to determine *the actual, not general* hazards that are found within your operations. As you become more versed in the practice of workplace safety management, you will agree that overcoming this hazard is essential.

Challenge 3: Recognizing the Need for Specific Safeguards and Controls

If you understand your operations and the hazards that are present, then you can define a specific course of action to control the hazards and implement safeguards. More important, the safeguards you adopt will be related to the unsafe acts and unsafe conditions you have identified.

Understanding operations, the nature of the hazards that emanate from them, and the controls necessary to keep them in check is a powerful tool in your workplace safety arsenal. If you can consistently make the connection between these three challenges and overcome of each, you will be well on your way to understanding and fending off Challenge 4.

Challenge 4: Putting a Workplace Safety Plan in Motion

Do not be lulled into inaction because you are new at workplace safety management or just getting started on your workplace safety program. Get the process rolling, obtain subject matter assistance from within the company, and go beyond talking about safety and start your program's tactical steps.

If need be, reach outside your organization to experts who may be available from your insurance broker or companies; many other sources exist as well. Oftentimes industry associations you belong to have resources you can call upon. As mentioned earlier, we caution against using someone else's plan; such plans rarely have any relationship to your operations and need significant editing. Borrowing a plan does nothing to assist in overcoming Challenges 1, 2, and 3. Roll your sleeves up and get at it.

The only way to ensure success when faced with Challenge 4 is to seek the appropriate approvals, where needed, put a team together, and establish meaningful time frames for completing the various elements of your plan. Write your own plan and conduct your own training; you will be glad you did. But do not wait. Start now and avoid the Churchill Paradox (discussed in the next section).

Note that the major challenges you face can be visualized as a cycle (see Exhibit 1.4).

Recognizing that one management activity precedes the other like a cycle is essential. Plans are not static. As new operations, machinery, and personnel are integrated and as new or revised regulations and the like become known, operations must be reassessed and plans modified. And it is very likely that, as the safety practitioner, you will have to go to the very first challenge and start again. So that you do not get shocked into inaction, it is important to note that, with practice, you will get better at managing these challenges.

Overcoming an Important Paradox

We end this first chapter with a philosophical thought that has proven meaningful to many people. To have any hope of developing a meaningful workplace safety program, you have to get at it. What do we mean by this? Let's use a story to make our point.

During the early stages of World War II and in spite of the urgings of Winston Churchill, the United States did not enter the war in Europe for quite some time. Churchill kept at it in 1939, 1940, and 1941, repeatedly asking the United States to get involved. However, having come through World War I not all that long before, our country was hesitant to enter another battle.

The United States engaged Germany in closed-door politicking, threatened military action and economic sanctions, and used diplomatic channels, all to no avail. Of course, once the United States did get involved in the European theater, the tide turned. Ultimately Hitler's forces were

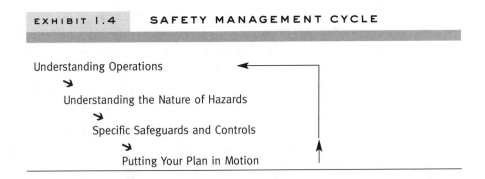

EXHIBIT 1.4   SAFETY MANAGEMENT CYCLE

Understanding Operations

↘
  Understanding the Nature of Hazards

  ↘
    Specific Safeguards and Controls

    ↘
      Putting Your Plan in Motion

turned back, and England and Europe were saved. As the United States was beginning its involvement, Winston Churchill, of course, had something to say about the country's actions and inactions. He has been quoted as saying:

> The Americans are a great people. You can always count on them to do the right thing . . . after they have tried everything else.

What's the relevance of this story to workplace safety management? Look at it this way: Churchill was imploring us to help very early in World War II, as he knew his country and most of Europe could not turn back the Nazi regime. They needed help from a growing superpower: the United States. It's likely we knew we were going to have to get involved but adopted an incremental approach instead. Of course, the Nazis marched on and millions died. Once we did engage, the threat to Europe was eventually controlled.

Much the same happens in the practice of workplace safety: We recognize a hazard or an adverse outcome, and instead of attacking it fully at the outset, we try several other steps first. Eventually we get it right, but while we are working toward getting it right, the hazards to employees continue, as do injuries and illnesses.

We call this approach to safety the Churchill Paradox. Overcoming the paradox and ensuring that the best workplace safety steps are implemented first will ultimately save you time, money, and the health of your workforce. Take the best actions first. Yes, sometimes you'll have to make an economic investment, but it will pay for itself many times over.

There is no doubt that you will face many challenges as you become more familiar with the management of workplace safety programs. The challenges are not insurmountable; in fact, you can consider them to represent an adventure that you will be glad you took. As you learn more about operations, you'll have an opportunity to interact with your organization's employees. While doing so, you'll develop credibility with them for your efforts. At the same time, you will become much more versed in the ways to control injuries and illnesses.

Taking Stock of Where You Are: A Needs Assessment

Before an organization can take stock of its workplace safety program, it must know how its program is structured and why it was so structured when it was first developed. We ask a few moments of patience as we explain several critical concepts, as we feel they will assist greatly in:

- Analyzing your program as it exists today
- Recognizing where improvements must be made
- Deploying a workplace safety program that has within it elements that are focused on the recognition of actual hazards, from both unsafe acts and conditions, and how best to control them

There has been a fundamental shift in what workplace safety programs are called. Some are referred to as injury and illness prevention programs, while others, especially historically, have been referred to as safety programs or accident prevention programs. What does this have to do with taking stock of where you are? You might be wondering.

Understanding what programs are called has everything to do with how an organization develops (writes, if you will) its workplace safety program and subsequently analyzes its effectiveness and other important characteristics, such as regulatory compliance. In addition, the program's name (title) plays a considerable role in the robustness and focus of an organization's plans.

The shift in terminology is certainly touched by a bit by academia, but as authors and teachers, we're okay with that. As practicing safety and health professionals, however, we also know that we have to find the practical discussion that works within industry and allows you, the person responsible for workplace safety, to recognize the value of what we're saying. In addition there is a practical aspect—that is, bettering your safety and health efforts by referring to your plan in a way that is meaningful to your company.

From the academic perspective, some of the changes in how safety programs are named have been based on research and the findings of those within the academic community. Other changes have been an outcome of the efforts of practitioners, and still other names come from terminologies contributed by the regulatory agencies that oversee safety and health performance within the business environment.

Twenty-five to thirty years ago, most plans were referred to as accident prevention plans. If you believe the definition of the word *accident* (a sudden, unforeseen event), then you will be able to recognize the hurdles people faced managing a program based around events that can't be explained. In the late 1960s and early 1970s, the term *safety programs* became common. This change occurred because the field was growing and the number of practitioners within workplace safety was increasing; many were tasked with the development of plans and programs. In many cases, effectiveness (at the time measured in reduced injuries and illnesses) was not the first measure of success.

Safety programs often focused on acute events that led to injuries and illnesses. This did not coincide with an ever-increasing understanding of the cumulative nature of some injuries and the fact that the practices of industrial hygiene and occupational medicine were hitting their strides. It would be nearly 20 years before there was significant focus on the fact that many processes resulted in not just injuries but illnesses as well, including those that were psychological (e.g., stress) or psychosocial (for example, some adverse outcomes from ergonomic-related stressors).

Today we see the consistent use of the term *injury and illness prevention programs* (IIPP). Use of the term IIPP suggests that both injuries and illnesses must be given equal consideration in programs focused on the welfare of workers. No longer are causes for any adverse outcome accepted as unknown (accidental). The outcomes are either injuries or illnesses, and they must develop from recognized exposures, whether physical, chemical, biological, ergonomic, or psychological.

Whether you title your program accident prevention, safety, safety and health, injury and illness prevention, or workplace safety, the reality is that it doesn't matter, unless there is a regulatory mandate to do so (which does exist in some states). What does matter is that your efforts recognize unsafe actions and conditions that contribute to both injuries and illnesses.

To summarize:

- Your workplace safety programs must recognize your employees' actual exposures.

- The program you develop must be capable of mitigating those exposures and ultimately the injuries and illnesses that may occur.

- Your analysis, regardless of the methodology employed, must be capable of analyzing exposures and outcomes.

As we move through this chapter and we refer to workplace safety programs, we ask that you think in terms of injury *and* illness prevention.

WHY WORKPLACE SAFETY PROGRAMS?

Thinking of your workplace safety program as an IIPP forces you into considering the exposures that result in both injuries and illnesses. Thus, when you begin taking stock of where your program is in its development and effectiveness, your analysis will be sufficiently robust.

From a workplace safety program perspective, you will be analyzing several critical characteristics and the capabilities of your program. A good starting point, regardless of the state you work within, will be to look up the OSHA program for your state. (The state plan directory can be found at www.osha.gov/fso/osp/ or www.workplacesafetynow.com.) Some states have specific programs (state OSHA programs); for other states, the federal OSHA (Fed/OSHA) program has been adopted or is in effect. Reviewing the applicable OSHA requirements will provide a fine baseline for you, but additional analysis is almost always required. In general, however, you will begin your analysis by looking at specifics within these general categories:

- Your organization's policy statement regarding safety and health management, including identification of responsible personnel
- Hazard recognition and resolution activities
- General rules and regulations or code of safe practices (specific safety codes and standards) that are operation- and hazard-specific
- Workplace safety communications
- Methods to evaluate, maintain, and improve your safety and health efforts and ensure compliance with your plan, including disciplinary capabilities
- Training and education programs that specifically support assisting employees in understanding the codes of safe practices, their roles and responsibilities toward safety, and the ramifications—from an injury development and administrative perspective—if they don't observe the practices (e.g., discipline)
- Tools required to manage safety and your program efforts, including recordkeeping

The fact that you have a workplace safety program is not an end all. It's what you accomplish with your safety program that makes all of the difference. Let's talk about some of the factors essential to workplace safety programs that should be kept in the forefront of your analytical efforts. These are the broad-scoped aspects (quantitative) of your analysis. We provide a program-specific example in this and the next chapters.

Quantitative Review Categories: Start Big!

- *Do you have to have a workplace safety program?* The easy answer is yes—every company needs a workplace safety program, but its detail and recordkeeping requirements may vary. OSHA may allow written plan exemptions (as for employers with a small number of employees or those in some non–high-hazard business sectors). Regardless of these exemptions, all employers should have a written plan. Some will be more comprehensive than others. From our perspective the safety and health of employees is too important to "wing it." OSHA provides sample programs for low-hazard employers with few employees that can help with program development (as long as specific hazard and operational modifications are incorporated). The answer to whether you must have a workplace safety program or plan is a simple one. Plan format and structure may be a bit tougher to analyze, however; we provide more detail on the structure in the following chapters.

- *Is your plan in the proper form or format?* Your plan should be in writing and, where necessary, it must be in languages or formats that all employees can understand. We've been to companies where plans were produced in English, Spanish, Tagolog, Hmong, Vietnamese, and Chinese, for example. If people are valued enough to be hired, then they should be valued enough to communicate with effectively. Does your plan provide for effective communication?

- *Do you understand or recognize the class of business you are in?* This is critical. Programs that are written for high-hazard operations, such as agriculture, construction, transportation, and many others, often must meet some specific requirements in their plan design, structure, and deployment. Make sure you know where you stand on this issue. Both Fed/OSHA and state OSHA programs define high-hazard industries. You can base some of the intricacies of your plan on these requirements. For example, there are specific requirements in addition to general industry standards for agriculture, construction, transportation, pressure vessels, elevators, and many more; your workplace safety program must be capable of recognizing the standards that apply and then integrating the proper general and specific industry safety practices.

- *Do you have the most frequent regulatory citations in mind as you develop your plan?* If you study and recognize the most frequent citations (published annually by the OSHA programs, the National Safety Council, some chambers of commerce, the Bureau of Labor Statistics, and other sources), then you will do a much better job of focusing your program efforts. Do you conduct this review? Some of the more common citations include no written workplace safety program, electrical hazards, recordkeeping violations, respiratory protection plan violations, and the lack of emergency action plans.

You can use this information to assist your organization in auditing and evaluating the safety and health function.

- *Is your workplace safety program sufficiently robust?* There is no one-size-fits-all plan. Certainly you've inferred that from previous comments. Merely having a written workplace safety program does not provide any guarantees that injuries and illnesses will be controlled, especially when hazard-specific codes of safe practice are missing. Your program must respond to the operations of your company and the hazards that are present. You may have only a few employees, but if these workers are steeplejacks, then your workplace safety program must be capable of addressing working at heights, fall protection, weather and temperature stresses, personal protective equipment, and many more considerations. The point here is that the fact that you have some written safety provisions should not give you total comfort. You must dig further and be certain that your plan can and does respond, through hazard recognition and control, to the actual hazards your employees face in their day-to-day tasks. Pound this point home every chance you get.

- *Do you recognize when your plans or workplace safety program should be reviewed and updated?* There are several ways to ensure that your plans are reviewed. One is simply to schedule annual reviews. However, other dynamics are indicative of the need to review your plan and ensure that it is current and effective. Some of the dynamics that stimulate these reviews include:

  - Scheduled reviews and audits
  - Changes in operations
  - Injury and illness trends: Is the plan reflective of how employees are becoming injured or ill?
  - New laws and regulations
  - New processes, materials, and equipment
  - Information provided by a worker, supervisor, or manager

There may be other triggers as well. Once they are identified, they should be added to your trigger list and, where necessary, be utilized to update your program.

These "big" categories are designed to get you to begin taking stock of where you are and where your program is in terms of its ability to assist in reducing injuries and illness, save the organization time, effort, and money, and assist with regulatory compliance.

Goals of Your Initial Assessment

The Society for Human Resources Management in a 2002 publication noted three specific and meaningful goals (paraphrased here) that OSHA has included in their efforts. It is worthwhile to reiterate these goals as you review or update your own plan:

Goal 1.   Improve workplace safety and health for all workers, as evidenced by fewer hazards, reduced exposures, and fewer injuries, illnesses, and fatalities.

Goal 2.   Change the workplace culture to increase employer and worker awareness of, commitment to, and involvement with safety and health. Toward this end, OSHA will make all standards, regulations, and reference materials available on the OSHA Web site.

Goal 3.   Secure public confidence through excellence in the development and delivery of OSHA's programs and services.

TAKING STOCK

OSHA's Goals Are Your Goals: Adopt This Philosophy When Taking Stock Of Your Program

OSHA's goals (or the state plan if you happen to work in a state that manages its own program) serve as the baseline for your goals and thus for how you actually review or audit your plans. There is, because of the way OSHA is structured, agreement between basic content requirements of the federal programs and state programs. We will discuss those here, but you should review both the federal and state-specific guidelines based on your organization's domicile.

As you begin your review, can you check off each one of the listed items as being present in your workplace safety program?

Every workplace safety program *must* contain these six core elements:

Management commitment and responsibility (how managers, supervisors, and employees are responsible for implementing the program and how continued participation of management will be established, measured, and maintained). Delineating management's commitment (in writing) to safety and health.

Employee involvement (and how safe work practices and rules will be enforced). Ensuring compliance among the workforce regarding codes of safe practice and any other safety and health procedures designed to safeguard their welfare.

Work-site analysis (the methods used to identify, analyze, and control new or existing hazards, conditions, and operations).

Hazard recognition and resolution (how workplace hazards are recognized and resolved, and how incidents will be investigated and corrective action implemented). Also includes incident investigations— the procedures for conducting the investigations and taking action on the findings.

Training and education (how the plan will be communicated to all affected employees so that they are informed of work-related hazards and controls). Provide for internal communications that highlight workplace hazards and applicable safety and health procedures.

Recordkeeping (maintain injury and illness, safety training, and inspection records).

Uncovering Management's Commitment: Your Assessment Requires Validation

Management demonstrates commitment to workplace safety programs and ensures the welfare of workers in several important ways. First, program efforts must be written, documented, and kept current. A written plan that is several years old and, more important, that does not recognize actual hazards in the workplace will hold no quarter with any OSHA (state or federal) compliance officer. This commitment is best demonstrated by including in the foreword to the workplace safety program two essential considerations: a *policy statement* in addition to the written comments concerning your (and management's) *commitment* to the safety and health of their employees. In all cases, this regulatory requirement must include an overview of the responsibilities of management, supervision, and employees alike. Again, the critical elements to ensure validated commitment are:

- An organizational policy statement regarding safety and health and the workplace safety program
- A statement from management regarding its commitment to safety
- A delineation of the responsibilities of management, supervision, and employees

Managers and supervisors have responsibilities unlike those of employees. It is within their function that plans are developed, maintained, implemented, and assurances made that all employees understand the workplace safety program.

Employee Involvement and Program Compliance

All workers, regardless of the role they occupy within an organization, must comply with both safety and health practices that have been made part of the workplace safety program. Your role is to ensure compliance, and there are several ways to do so. These methods include (but are not limited to):

- Instructing workers on the workplace safety program and its intent, content, and the role they play in its success.
- Observing work practices to ensure safe work procedures are being followed. (This requirement can be completed through scheduled inspections or during the normal course of business. As unsafe actions are noted, they must be corrected.)
- Initiating additional training activities where safety performance by employees is found to be unsafe or unacceptable.
- Disciplining employees for disregarding safety procedures or consistently working in an unsafe fashion.
- Positively recognizing those who exemplify safe work practices.

Work-Site Analysis: Identification and Assessment of Hazards

For most work sites, hazard identification involves conducting hazard inspections and reviewing related literature, such as material safety data sheets (MSDSs) and hazard information provided by manufacturers and distributors of equipment, materials, and process-related devices. What is most important to understand when considering hazard identification is that you are not limited to inspection checklists. Checklists, however, are important tools to a successful workplace safety program. In addition, use of the World Wide Web can be beneficial and, in certain cases, time-saving.

Although frequent and scheduled inspections are essential and required, remember that they should not be too general. In some cases, specific checklists need to be constructed for certain operations. As an example, use of a variety of metalworking equipment or certain chemicals would certainly require specific checklists. Fed/OSHA and/or your state OSHA program can provide an excellent example and starting point, should such a program be needed at your organization.

Hazard assessments should be conducted (your program assessment should include an analysis of whether these elements are recognized and complied with):

- When a program is initiated (sets the baseline).

- When injuries have occurred.

- When there has been process, equipment, or material changes.

- When employees have informed you of unsafe acts or conditions.

- When it is suspected that personal protective equipment needs to be introduced. Conducting a thorough hazard assessment is essential toward ensuring the proper safety equipment is obtained.

- When required based on a compliance or consultation audit by the applicable OSHA agency.

- When you learn of hazards in similar businesses through associations, industry groups, the popular media, and so on. We refer to this as hazard recognition by analogy. The implication here is that you should not be surprised by too much!

Hazard Recognition and Resolution

As an employer or the person responsible for safety and health activities, heed the warning: "If it's not in writing, it did not happen."

Yes, this is a generalization for the need to document your workplace safety efforts. Documentation is extremely important when considering safe practices (especially when they change), hazard inspections/assessments, and incident investigations. It is equally important to document improvements and changes made as a result of inspections (referred to as hazard management activities). The soundest ways to ensure documentation is to build the requirement into your plan, add such requirements to a calendaring or diary system, and make documentation an essential component of your program audit activities. In other words:

- Ensure documentation of hazard correction and control activities.
- Include a section in your workplace safety program to help with such documentation.
- Occasionally audit the documentation and validation efforts of your firm.

Incident Investigations

Conducting incident investigations demonstrates meaningful management commitment toward employee safety and health. Incident investigations are one of the safety practitioner's finest tools. To be in compliance with regulations, incident investigations must be conducted in a timely fashion and in writing, and unsafe acts/conditions that are discovered must be corrected.

There is tremendous value in investigating near misses in addition to actual injuries and illnesses. Frequent "minor events" are clear evidence that a serious event is on the horizon. Additionally, incident investigations must be completed by those trained in the processes and those that understand your organization's operations. Using trained and competent personnel also helps ensure that corrective action requirements are both valid and can be accomplished. Consider these questions as you analyze your program efforts:

- Does your firm conduct incident investigations?
- Are near misses reviewed and investigated?
- Are those responsible for conducting incident investigations trained in the processes?

Training, Education, and Communication

Business managers can ensure (and are held accountable for) responsible communication with workers regarding hazards, safe work procedures, and their responsibilities toward adhering to these practices. For example, here are six ways employers can comply with the communication requirement:

- New worker orientation, including a discussion of safety and health policies and procedures
- Review of the workplace safety program with employees—ensuring that all questions are answered
- Training programs—both general and specific hazard-related
- Regularly scheduled general safety meetings as well as those that may be issue-specific
- Posted or distributed safety information
- System for workers to inform management anonymously about workplace hazards and unsafe acts

You should ensure that communications are in a readily understood form and that all employees recognize that they can report unsafe acts and conditions to management without fear of reprisal. The phrase *readily understood* will take on several different meanings based on the makeup of your workforce. Different languages may apply. Some employees may require assistance with the use of pictograms if language barriers exist. If you employ hearing-impaired persons, for example, you will need to consider the use of American Sign Language within your program.

Safety- and Health-Related Training

As a trainers and educators, we are biased toward this requirement—always have been, always will be! However, we learned very early in our careers that two critical dynamics exist that you should be aware of:

1. Most employers, in their efforts to comply with the regulation related to safety and health training, actually are providing education, not training. The distinction between the two bears repeating. When you say you are providing training, then train! Training is hands-on. Training is task- and job-specific. Training is specific to safe work practices and, most important, training has an observable, validated feedback mechanism.

Think of it this way. If you have operations that require the use of a self-contained breathing apparatus (SCBA), are you going to rely on educating (say, through the use of a video) workers or training workers on the uses, hazards, and safeguards while using SCBAs? Of course not, you'll train. Employees will have to demonstrate they can don and doff the SCBA, that they can read the gauges properly, and that they know how to activate and utilize emergency oxygen canisters.

This demonstration is not only essential toward complying with regulations, it is likely essential to the safety and, possibly, the life of a worker. If you only provide education, or stop at it, employees will not have learned the applied aspects of using SCBAs. Many sound training efforts begin with education activities, but they do not end there.

2. Do a brief survey of two to three years' history of completed incident investigations. How many of them indicate, as the corrective action, that more training is needed? Ten percent, 20 percent, more? Probably a number of them refer to training as the corrective action, when in fact such efforts might be only part of the solution or not at all. As young safety professionals, we learned that "You cannot train away the woes [incidents, unsafe acts and conditions, and injuries and illnesses] of the world."

    Training may help. However, often the solution to a hazard rests with improving processes, repairing equipment, adding guards to machines, and ensuring that proper employees are assigned to specific tasks or jobs. Sometimes resolving woes requires a decision to abandon a particularly unsafe activity. Though rare, such an action might be necessary.

Here are a few triggers as to when training should be provided. Make these part of your workplace safety program and your program analysis, and expand them where you think they can be beneficial. Remember, training applies to management and supervising personnel as well. Provide training:

- When a workplace safety program is first established.
- To all new workers. (There may be some modifications for construction workers.)
- To all workers given new job assignments for which training has not been previously provided.

- Whenever new substances, processes, procedures, or equipment are introduced to the workplace and represent a new hazard. (You'll need to develop a mechanism with other departments, such as receiving a copy of all new material safety data sheets when introduced).

- Whenever you are made aware of a new or previously unrecognized hazard—including through anonymous reports by employees. (Consider installing a safety suggestion box.)

- To supervisors to familiarize them with the safety and health hazards to which workers under their immediate direction and control may be exposed and to ensure that they can provide appropriate training themselves.

- To all workers with respect to hazards specific to each employee's job assignment.

- Subsequent to injuries/illnesses.

Recordkeeping

Recordkeeping requirements pertain to the analysis, documentation, publication, submission in some cases (to OSHA agencies and/or the Bureau of Labor Statistics), of injury and illness records (including what are referred to as exposure records).

Basic recordkeeping requirements are found within OSHA (or the applicable state OSHA program) guidelines and are focused on three basic reports that (most) employers must complete and retain. These basic forms include the:

Form 300: Log of Work-Related Injuries and Illnesses

Form 300A: Summary of Work-Related Injuries and Illnesses

Form 301: Injuries and Illnesses Incident Report

Examples of the forms are provided for your reference in the Selected References and Resources at the end of the book and online at www.workplacesafetynow.com. These forms can be requested from your local OSHA office and perhaps your workers' compensation insurance carrier. The easiest way to obtain the recordkeeping forms is via the Web.

Do not view these forms as simply a repository for injury and illness information. Although their completion and retention is critical to regulatory compliance, the information contained within the forms is much more valuable in your program efforts. Injury and illness trends, location of incidents, and temporal information, such as time of day and day of the week, are captured as well. This information can assist you in focusing your corrective action efforts.

Form 300 provides event-specific information that should serve as a trigger for task or process improvement whenever possible. At the very least, you should ask the question "Can I improve this process, use a less hazardous substance, or perhaps not use it at all?" regularly. Doing so is another hallmark of a safety practitioner.

Form 300A, the Summary of Work-Related Injuries and Illnesses, must be posted each year, where all employees can review it if desired. Posting periods have been extended over the past few years and now run from February 1 to April 30 of each year, for the previous year's statistics.

Form 301 is the Injuries and Illnesses Incident Report (not an incident investigation), and the information found on this form assists with the completion of Form 300. Form 301 must, for example, be completed within seven days of a recordable injury or illness and must further be maintained for five years following the year to which it pertains. (Consider this retention requirement a minimum. In certain health exposure cases, retention requirements may be considerable longer.) Exposure records that pertain to certain toxic substances and other hazardous exposures require that this information, as well as other sources, physical examination reports, and employment records, be retained for considerably longer periods. Such records usually pertain to exposure to carcinogens, or other chemical, physical or biological exposures.

Federal OSHA and state OSHA Web sites, in conjunction with internal or external legal counsel, are the best resources for determining your record retention requirements. (The major differences, for example, in California and Fed/OSHA recordkeeping requirements can be found at www.dir.ca.gov/dosh/dosh-publications/cal-fed.)

As an employer, are you complying with:

- Updating the OSHA Forms 300, 300A, and 301 as required?

- Posting the summary document from February 1 to April 30 of each year?

- Maintaining documents in accordance with mandatory record retention requirements?

Specific Safety and Health Concerns

Many workplace safety programs fall short not only in complying with applicable regulations but in the recognition and control of specific hazards. Most employers do a fine job of recognizing general hazards, such as slippery surfaces, sharp materials, and many ergonomic hazards. There are, of course, a myriad of exposures in a working establishment that are not general but rather very specific in nature. That is, hazards that are specifically related to the use of a tool, machine or process. Their safety controls, then, are, specific, not general.

Chapter 4 discusses many of the hazards that must be included in workplace safety programs. Your analysis must include:

- A review of specific safety and health concerns
- Recognizing whether processes, information, and tools exist to conduct hazard-specific analyses

Ancillary Considerations

As you endeavor to structure or enhance existing workplace safety programs, you should be aware of several ancillary considerations, including:

- *The development and retention of new employee safety and health orientation checklists.* Such checklists are often completed and entered into an employees' human resources (HR) file. These checklists validate critical information. Be cautious against checking boxes that suggest all safety and health or special hazard protection training has been provided, when in fact it hasn't. Additionally, it is traditional that employees are provided an opportunity to sign such forms. It is, or will be, your responsibility to ensure that employees understand the orientation checklist and what they are signing.

- *Safety committee meetings.* To everyone's surprise, such meetings are not (always) a required workplace safety program element. Although they are an excellent program adjunct and we highly recommend that every employer use these meetings, they may not be required for your operations. However, if a safety committee is part of your workplace safety program efforts, certain minimum requirements apply. These requirements include:

- Committees must include labor and management representatives.
- Committees should meet regularly, but no less often than quarterly.
- Committees need to prepare and make available to employees written records of the meetings. Further, these records need to be retained for agency (e.g., OSHA) review when requested.
- Committee activities must include a review of injuries and illnesses, trends, and related incident investigations. Recommendations to management regarding corrective action and hazard prevention suggestions are an important part of the committee's duties.
- Committee members who have been advised of unsafe acts or conditions will bring those concerns to the full committee for review and resolution.

Other benefits of safety committees include, but are not necessarily part of the regulatory demands:

- Committees serve as an excellent training ground for future safety and health practitioners within your organization.
- Committees and committee members tend to valuable contributors to your safety and health training efforts.
- Committee members often are a valuable resource for performing hazard inspections and recommending practical solutions to both unsafe acts and conditions.
- Committees on the whole or selected committee members can play an essential role in assisting you in completing program audits or reviews.

We highly recommend the development, use, and maintenance of a workplace safety program activity calendar. These calendars, such as the example found in the Selected References and Resources, can help keep track of meetings, safety and health training, inspection schedules, new employee orientation sessions, specific hazard program element reviews, and many other scheduled activities.

If you adopt the use of such a calendar, it is essential that it be maintained. Changes in operations, personnel, equipment, processes and the like, are all triggers to review and update the calendar. The calendars are an excellent tool and we have found that many organizations choose to copy these calendars for all of their departments or in a large size format, for all staff members to be able to view. Finally, the calendars are a gentle reminder when you might get behind on your safety activities and can help you get back on track with important activities.

Program Audits

In both the short and the long run, program audits are very important. Your initial program development efforts will create a baseline, and regular audits will be an indicator of the success, or lack thereof, of your activities.

Many insurance companies, brokers, and other consultants can provide you with various models. Of course, our desire is that you will take the time to create your own—you will benefit from this organic process. Your audit will be more specific and reflect your workplace safety program's structure and goals.

There are, however, advantages to outside audits. Safety and health professionals with more experience and skill than you can perform the audit. Just as important, these reviews carry less institutional bias.

An example safety program audit summary rating page (see Exhibit 2.1) is provided as background. Take the time to create an audit and an audit evaluation scale. Where time commitment and cost is acceptable, perform both an internal and external audit and compare the results. If you decide to adopt the format shown, be certain to modify the form to fit your specific program. Of course, you'll need to develop the audit questions for each of the sections. (This is an excellent project for the safety committee team members.) You can certainly use the Taking Stock Comprehensive Checklist (see the Appendix) and use this as the basis for your program audit.

For example (and in general), one of the first documents that should be reviewed is the facility's Log of Work-Related Injuries and Illnesses (OSHA Form 300). The log and the accompanying first report of injury forms should be examined for trends, such as similar injuries to those workers with similar job duties, similar causes of injuries and illnesses, or departments with higher-than-average injury rates. Incident investigation reports should also be reviewed. If similar incidents or near misses continue to occur in the facility, perhaps the root causes of the events are not being determined during the investigation or corrective action is not being implemented.

EXHIBIT 2.1   SAMPLE AUDIT SUMMARY PAGE

Annual Program Audit—Summary Rating

Organization: _____

Department (if applicable): _____

Department/Function: _____

Date: _____

Completed by: _____

Category

Poor	0–1+
Fair	2–5+
Good	6–8+
Excellent	9–10

Comments on Rating

1. Workplace safety program
2. Standard operating procedures or risks
3. Safety responsibilities
4. Group safety talks
5. Inspections
6. Training
7. Incident reporting and investigation
8. Housekeeping
9. Emergency procedures
10. Safety committees
11. Equipment/tool use and maintenance
12. Personal protective equipment
13. Material handling
14. Chemical safety/hazard communication
15. Noise control
16. Fleet operations
17. Employee orientation
18. Employee placement

Continues

EXHIBIT 2.1   *Continued*

19. Return to work for injured employees
20. Supervisor safety responsibilities
21. Employee safety responsibilities
22. First aid

Total points: _____

(Previous points: _____)

Date: _____

Discussion:

Reports from safety committees, supervisor inspections, or walk-arounds should be reviewed as well. If the hazards causing injury or illness in the workplace are not being identified through these inspections, then efforts should be made to assist the individuals to improve the reporting process. Possibilities include additional training about hazard recognition; technical assistance from a workplace safety consultant, insurance loss-control specialist, or private consultant; or the allotment of more time for more extensive or frequent inspections. Corrective actions resulting from hazards identified during incident investigations or routine inspections should be taken as soon as possible. Specific written programs, such as "Employee Right to Know" and "Respiratory Protection," should also be reviewed for completeness and accuracy.

Employee and supervisor interviews are the next step. These can be conducted formally or can be a simple casual conversation as part of an inspection or walk-around. Employees should be selected at random for the interviews. If you use contract employees, they should be interviewed as well. Some of the questions asked should include:

- What are some of the hazards involved with your job? How do you protect yourself from them?

- Are there any written operating procedures? If so, are they correct? Do you follow them as written? Describe the safety precautions you follow.

- What are your responsibilities for workplace safety?
- Do you know what the organization's goals are for workplace safety and health? What are they?
- What are the chemicals that you work with? What are some of the possible health effects if you are overexposed to them?
- Do you have any specific safety and health concerns? What are they?
- Do you know how to report a safety hazard so that it can be corrected? How?
- Are safety hazards corrected when you point them out to your supervisor or manager? If not, why?
- Do you know how to evacuate the area in case of fire or other emergency? What are your escape routes?
- Do you know where to go to get replacements for worn or dirty personal protective equipment? Where?
- How are safety rules enforced?

Simple observation can be an important evaluation tool. By walking around the facility, you can pick up clues about whether the safety and health program is working. Some items to check for include:

- Are aisles and exits clear of boxes, raw material, refuse, and so on?
- Are guards in place, or have they been removed from the machines?
- Are employees wearing the correct personal protective equipment?

Closing Thoughts

Whether you are in New York, California, or Hawaii, certain program or workplace safety program requirements apply. Call your program whatever you like (though the regulatory agencies like to see their terms utilized), but be certain that you meet the regulatory mandates. Some of you may have operations in different jurisdictions, so picking the most stringent state required program may cover the needs of all of your locations. For instance, California's workplace safety program requirements are very rigorous. To assume, however, that a given state's regulations are applicable to all of your operations will catch you flat-footed sooner or later. Compare all jurisdictions requirements, build a basic core plan, and then amend that plan as necessary.

Workplace safety programs can be your friend; treat them like one! You must analyze their capabilities, and doing so should become part of your regular safety and health activities. Take stock of where you are now, enhance your program where necessary, and then keep it up to date and in compliance with regulations at all times. More important, be sure that your program actually recognizes and responds to unsafe acts and conditions that are found within your operations. If you identify and control hazards, you will be well on your way to regulatory compliance and keeping all of your employees safe and productive.

CHAPTER 3

Creating an Effective Workplace Safety Program

The goal of an effective workplace safety program is the development of a long-term plan that is successful in protecting people from injury or worse, complying with regulations, and controlling the associated financial costs of loss. An effective plan must include methods to:

- Identify and understand all hazards, real and potential
- Prevent and control hazards so workers are not exposed or the exposure is minimized

Our goal is to help you create your workplace safety program—one that protects your people, saves you money, and complies with the law. We also recognize the importance of providing templates and resources to make the building of your workplace safety program a smooth process. In addition to the Selected References and Resources section at the back of this book, we have created an online resource page with sample workplace safety programs and other templates at www.workplacesafetynow.com.

CORE REGULATORY REQUIREMENTS[1]

Sound safety leadership results in prevention and control of employee injuries, exposures to toxic substances, and other unhealthful conditions (which can produce work-related illnesses). Effective workplace safety systems produce lower costs, higher productivity, reduced waste, and improved employee morale.

In an effort to help you create an effective workplace safety program, we have reviewed each state and federal safety program requirement and combined those guidelines and regulations with best practices learned over many years.

Although workplace safety programs go by different names, each state requires that there be a *written workplace safety program* (injury and illness prevention and reduction program) that promotes safety and healthful working conditions. An employer must conduct and document a review of the workplace safety program at least annually and document how procedures set forth in the program are met. In addition, all training and communication must be in a language that your employees understand. To facilitate this diversity, many companies translate their programs to accommodate their workforce.

For clarification, we often use words such as *management, managers,* and *supervisors.* We recognize that in a small company, there may be just one person (you) in a "management" role.

A little later in this chapter, and then again in Chapter 7, we discuss the significance of and methods involved in making safety a core value (there is a difference between making safety a *value* versus a priority) in your company. In addition to the importance of identifying safety as a company value, your written workplace safety program *must* contain these core elements:

- *Management commitment and responsibility* (how managers, supervisors, and employees are responsible for implementing the program and how continued participation of management will be established, measured, and maintained). This section delineates management's commitment (in writing) to safety and health.

- *Employee involvement* (and how safe work practices and rules will be enforced). This section discusses ensuring compliance among the workforce regarding codes of safe practice and any other safety and health procedures designed to safeguard their welfare.

- *Work-site analysis* (the methods used to identify, analyze, and control new or existing hazards, conditions, and operations).

- *Hazard recognition and resolution* (how workplace hazards are recognized and resolved, and how incidents will be investigated and corrective action implemented.) This section also includes incident investigations, the procedures for both conducting the investigations and taking action on the findings.

- *Training and education* (how the plan will be communicated to all affected employees so that they are informed of work-related hazards and controls). This section provides for internal communications that highlight workplace hazards and applicable safety and health procedures.

- *Recordkeeping* (the maintaining of injury and illness, safety training, and inspection records).

Program Review

As discussed in Chapter 2, an employer must conduct and document a review of the workplace safety program at least annually and document how procedures set forth in the program are met. Program review is vital because it serves as a check to see if the organization is making progress toward its goal of creating a safer, healthier workplace for all employees.

The second reason for conducting a review or audit of the workplace safety program is to determine whether the procedures used in the facility or operations are consistent with those described in the program.

The primary focus of the annual evaluation effort should be to determine whether the organization has made progress in achieving the workplace safety program's goals and objectives within the past year and, if so, whether the progress made actually *improved worker safety and health*. If an organization has achieved the goals and objectives described in its safety and health program, it should set new goals and objectives for the coming year to further improve safety and health on the job. The organization, its management, and its employees should work continually to improve workplace safety, just as they do to improve quality, cost effectiveness, and other facets of the business.

If an organization is not meeting its objectives, especially the ones established specifically for the previous year, it needs to determine why. Perhaps the organization is improving and moving toward its goal but just has not reached it yet. Timelines should be established or reestablished for each of the objectives and the overall goals. If progress is not being made or is being made too slowly, the goals and objectives need to be examined. Perhaps the goals and objectives are not clear or measurable. Objectives should be clear, concise, and capable of being measured or demonstrated. New objectives may need to be created that act as measurable steps toward achieving the greater goals. Not meeting objectives may also indicate that there are problems (sometimes serious) with the overall safety and health program that need to be addressed.

In addition to the needs assessment and taking stock from Chapter 2, the first step in a program evaluation should be to review the documentation created during the past year relevant to the workplace safety and health program.

Completing the Program Review

After the evaluation process is completed, the workplace safety program should be updated to correct shortfalls, and new goals should be set for the organization. Responsibility for making the program changes should be assigned to a specific person or persons, and implementation or due dates should be specified to ensure that the program is updated in a timely manner. Finally, changes to the program, goals, and procedures need to be communicated to everyone within the organization.

While the laws require that workplace safety programs be reviewed at least annually, ideally the program should be referred to, reviewed, and updated as necessary. This keeps the program fresh, accurate, and an integral part of the organization.

ESTABLISHING GOALS

Central to a successful workplace safety program are the *goals and objectives* an organization sets for its overall safety and health program.

Goals establish the direction for the program and state what the organization wants to achieve through it. The best goals are generally challenging to reach or complete but are also possible to achieve. They should be specific to the organization or facility.

Objectives are the specific actions that will be taken to attempt to achieve the goals. The best objectives are those that can either be measured or demonstrated.

Ideally, safety and health programs should correspond with and become part of the organization's overall mission or business plan. Every employee should know what the goals of the organization's safety program are and how they are to be achieved.

Some examples of goals and objectives are:

Goal 1

- We will reduce our injury and illness rate by 15 percent by 2008, using 2005 as the baseline.

Objectives

- We will address all employee safety issues in a timely manner; that is, hazards that potentially pose an imminent danger of death or serious physical injury will be addressed initially within one shift, and other hazards will be addressed initially within one week.
- We will perform a monthly safety inspection of all departments and will take corrective action or begin investigating long-term solutions for all hazards identified during the inspection within one week.
- We will investigate all incidents and near-miss events and will take corrective action within 24 hours to prevent a recurrence.

Goal 2

- We will establish and maintain a company culture that is committed to workplace safety and health.

Objectives

- We will conduct regular safety meetings on a quarterly basis to inform employees about specific workplace safety and health issues and to build an overall awareness of employee safety and health.
- We will actively enforce all safety rules throughout the company.
- Our facility will apply for a state or federal voluntary protection program status by the end of 2008.

SAFETY AS A COMPANY VALUE

In addition to core regulatory requirements, and the strong link between active workplace safety programs and low rates of occupational injury and illness, we advocate that you make employee safety and health an *intrinsic company value* (that working safe is not just a "program," but a way of doing things).

Ideally, safety and health programs should correspond with and become part of the organization's overall mission or business plan. Every employee should know what the goals of the organization's safety program are and how they are to be achieved.

Safety must be integrated as an *intrinsic company value* (not a priority) among every leader, manager, and employee in the organization. Safety should be viewed as a value just like honesty, working hard, and showing up to work on time. Values are embedded; priorities can change. Making safety a company value leads to building a workplace safety culture.

We create a *workplace safety culture* by (1) making safety part of the performance appraisal process, (2) practicing "actively caring" techniques, (3) engaging employees at all levels, and (4) having company leaders, managers, and employees commit to being safe. An organization should *expect* its leaders, managers, and people to make safety a value.

MANAGEMENT COMMITMENT AND RESPONSIBILITY

Your participation and commitment is crucial to the success of the workplace safety program. You must not only establish the program and communicate it to everyone within the organization, but you must also provide the resources to improve safety and health throughout the entire organization. Doing this includes providing employees and supervisors with the authority to identify and correct hazards, the budget to purchase new equipment or make repairs, the training necessary to work safely and to recognize hazards, and the systems to get repairs made, materials ordered, and other improvements accomplished.

As a business owner and manager, you also establish the importance of the workplace safety program, both by the priority you give workplace safety and health issues, and by the example you set by initiating safety and health improvements, correcting hazards, enforcing safety rules, rewarding excellent performance in safety and health, and following all safety rules. (Think about the message it sends when "the boss" walks through the shop without safety glasses when everyone else has to wear them.)

Safety and health programs are similar to quality improvement and other efforts organizations engage in to continually improve performance, customer service, competitiveness, organizational culture, and so forth.

In a small to medium-size business, employees will reflect the safety attitudes of its leaders and managers. If the organization is not interested in preventing employee injury and illness, employees probably will not give safety and health much thought. Therefore, it is absolutely essential that leaders and managers in an organization demonstrate at all times their personal concern for employee safety and health. An organization's actions and policies must clearly demonstrate that safety is an *intrinsic company value*.

Workplace safety programs must describe how everyone in the organization, whether management, first-line supervision, or labor, is responsible for making the program work. These duties should be clearly laid out. Everyone in the organization should be able to explain what their role is in creating a safer, healthier workplace.

Employees should feel they have some ownership and responsibility for creating a safe workplace. They should also be provided with the training, equipment, resources, and assistance to carry out their roles. Employees and supervisors need to know where to go to obtain assistance to resolve issues of safety and health concerns and to get questions answered. Most important, they need to know how to correct safety and health hazards in the workplace as the hazards are identified.

Some examples of assigned responsibilities are:

For Everyone in the Organization:

- All employees, including supervisors and managers, follow all safety rules at all times.

For Employees:

- Promptly report any safety and health hazards they observe to you or their supervisor.
- Perform each job task safely. If employees are unsure how to perform the task safely, they must consult with their supervisor.
- Wear personal protective equipment (PPE) as required for their protection, and maintain the equipment in a sanitary manner.

- Report all incidents, including near misses, to their supervisor immediately upon occurrence.

For Supervisors:

- Discuss any current safety issues with employees at the beginning of all regularly scheduled meetings.
- Address all safety concerns raised by staff members by initially investigating the issue, determining if the concern is valid, and taking appropriate corrective action whenever necessary. Corrective action can include:
  - Ordering new equipment
  - Issuing maintenance work orders
  - Consulting with an outside expert
- After an injury, initiate an incident investigation and submit the completed incident investigation report.
- Actively and positively participate in all safety inspections, training, and enforcement activities.
- Conduct monthly meetings and area inspections to review incident reports, identify hazards, and address any and all safety concerns raised by employees.
- Review the workplace safety program at least annually, and make recommendations concerning updates and revisions to ownership/management.
- Address all safety concerns brought to them by their employees and coworkers.

For Management:

- Communicate to all employees and supervisors the importance of worker safety and health throughout the organization.
- Review all safety concerns brought forward by first-line supervisors and employees.
- Review the workplace safety program and any recommended revisions from supervisors and employees at least annually, make the

appropriate revisions, and work with supervisors and employees to communicate the revisions.

- Review all incident investigation reports and take appropriate action to prevent recurrence.

- Conduct, in cooperation with first-line supervisors, all safety training required by regulation or identified as a need to assure a safe workplace.

- Make improvements in physical plant, machinery, equipment, raw materials, and PPE.

Leaders and managers must understand their safety and health responsibilities and roles.

Enforcement of Workplace Safety Programs

Responsibility for safety and health exists at all levels in an organization. Owners, managers, supervisors, and employees all should know what their duties are to create a safe and healthful workplace and must follow all safety rules. All employees must know and understand what they need to do and what they need not to do to make the workplace safer for themselves and their coworkers. Workers must be trained about safe work practices and proper use of engineering controls and PPE. Additional strategies to enforce safety include:

- Coach employees to correct unsafe actions and discipline them if violations continue. Safety procedures should become a key part of the daily routine.

- Enforce safety rules. Supervisors are responsible for ensuring that engineering controls and PPE are correctly used and that procedures are followed correctly. Supervisors should be taught basic skills in being an effective supervisor.

- Support and encourage supervisors who attempt to enforce the rules fairly and equally. Safe work practice rules are not effective if their use is not enforced. Typically, OSHA holds the employer responsible if the organization does not enforce its own rules. Many supervisors do not like to discipline employees, especially if the employees are generally good workers. Others may not feel that management backs them when they take disciplinary action against employees. If workplace rules are not enforced, they cease to have meaning.

- Enforce safe work practices. Such enforcement should be fair and consistent throughout the organization and based on an established policy.

- Set and obey the same rules as the rest of the workforce. Management and supervisors should be conscious of the examples they set for the workplace.

- Recognize exceptional workplace safety and health performance.

EMPLOYEE INVOLVEMENT

Leaders and managers can demonstrate their depth of safety commitment by involving employees in the planning and delivery of workplace safety. Employees who are involved in the identification and resolution of safety and health problems bring their unique insights and energy to achieving the organization's safety goals and objectives. Doing this also creates employee safety buy-in and safety ownership. Employees are among the most valuable asset you have, and their safety, health, and goodwill are essential to the success of your business. Asking your employees to cooperate with you in protecting their safety and health not only helps to keep them healthy; it makes your job easier. Here are some actions to consider to engage your workforce:

- Post the organization's safety and health policy next to the OSHA workplace poster where all employees can see it.

- Hold a meeting with all employees to communicate the workplace safety policy, and discuss objectives for safety and health.

- Make sure that your support is visible by getting personally involved in the activities that are part of the safety and health program. Ensure that all leaders, managers, and supervisors follow *all safety requirements* that apply to all employees (e.g., if an area requires a hard hat, safety glasses, and/or safety shoes, everyone in management must wear them when in the area, even if only briefly). If you run an administrative office or department, practice good ergonomics. We have known presidents and owners of large companies to become personally involved (supportive) when a person has suffered an injury.

- Take advantage of employees' specialized knowledge and encourage them to buy into the program by having them make inspections, conduct safety training, or investigate incidents.

- Make clear assignments of responsibility for every part of the organization's safety and health program, and make sure everyone understands them. The more people who are involved, the better. A good rule of thumb is to assign safety and health responsibilities in the same way production responsibilities are assigned.

- Make working safely a part of everyone's job.

- Give those with safety and health responsibility enough people, time, training, money, and authority to fulfill their role.

- After assignments are made, make sure the job gets done.

- Recognize those who do well and correct those who don't.

- At least once a year, review accomplishments and reevaluate whether new objectives or program revisions are needed.

- Institute an accountability system where all employees will be held accountable for safety.

In small companies, everyone may be part of an informal safety committee, where employees participate in various safety activities and responsibilities. However, some states require all employers with more than a certain number of employees (or at a certain injury rate) to establish a safety committee (also known as joint labor-management safety committee). Whether in a small or large company, typically these committees:

- Hold regularly scheduled meetings (unless otherwise provided in a collective bargaining agreement)

- Consist of volunteers, although in some states members must be selected by employees

An active, trained safety committee can be an important tool for implementing an effective workplace safety program. Duties that safety committee members can assume include:

- Participating in regular safety inspections

- Training new employees about safe working procedures

- Performing job hazard analyses or job safety analyses

- Providing input for the creation of workplace safety and health rules
- Presenting safety and health information at regularly scheduled staff meetings
- Assisting in incident investigations
- Bringing employee safety and health concerns and complaints to the attention of supervisors for correction

Safety committee members should be able/allowed to perform their safety duties without fear of discrimination or retaliation by management.

WORK-SITE ANALYSIS

As reviewed in the Chapter 2, we encourage readers to use a needs assessment tool (also see Selected References and Resources) to help identify physical hazards and unsafe work practices.

It is your responsibility to know what items or substances are in the workplace that could harm your people. Work-site analysis is a group of processes that helps you understand what's needed to keep workers safe. Some items to consider are:

- Request a consultation visit from your state on-site consultation program covering both safety and health to get a full survey of the hazards that exist in your workplace and those that could develop.
- Contact your workers' compensation insurance carrier—some companies offer a safety and health walk-through and provide recommendations.
- Contract services from expert private consultants.
- Establish a way to obtain professional advice when you make changes to procedures or equipment, to ensure that the changes are not introducing new hazards into the workplace.
- Find ways to keep current on newly recognized hazards in your industry (associations, hard-copy and digital newsletters, and e-groups).
- Periodically review with employees each job, analyzing it step-by-step to see if there are any hidden hazards in the equipment or procedures.
- Set up a self-inspection system to check your hazard controls and evaluate any new hazards.

- Make sure employees feel comfortable in alerting you when they see things that look dangerous or out of place.

- Learn how to conduct a thorough investigation when things go wrong. This will help you develop ways to prevent recurrences.

- Review your company's injury and illness records from previous years to identify patterns that may help you devise strategies to improve workplace safety and health. Periodically review several months of records to determine if any new patterns are developing. In small companies, there may be no injuries for review; however, there may be near misses, or identified hazards that can be identified.

HAZARD RECOGNITION AND RESOLUTION

Hazard recognition and resolution is another core aspect of your workplace safety program. It includes both hazards that currently exist in the workplace and those that may occur due to future changes, such as the introduction of new equipment, processes, or materials or the revision of existing procedures.

Hazard Recognition

Organizations can use several methods to identify hazards. Some rely solely on walk-around inspections by first-line supervisors, management, or safety committees and employees; others involve formal hazard analyses of different parts of the operation; still others use a combination of methods. Regardless of the methods used, the best hazard identification methods combine expert opinion about safety and health hazards with input from either a cross-disciplinary team or at least one employee who works directly with the process or equipment in question. At least some of the individuals involved in hazard identification should be trained in hazard recognition.

Inspections should be made on a regular basis to identify both newly developed hazards and those previously missed. In certain environments, you should also consider the value of periodic industrial hygiene monitoring and sampling for hazardous substances, noise, and heat.

Checklists are one of the more common tools used for hazard identification. Examples can be found in the Selected References and Resources (or at www.workplacesafe tynow.com). Checklists serve as a good starting point for organizations to assist employers and employees identify workplace hazards. One disadvantage of using a checklist is that it focuses an inspection on certain specific hazards and can cause other hazards not on the checklist to go unnoticed. This is particularly true of generic checklists that are not site- or process-specific.

A method often used to identify workplace hazards is job hazard analysis (JHA), also known as job safety analysis (JSA). Job hazard analysis is a step-by-step method of identifying the hazards associated with a particular task or job. It is important to involve the employee who normally performs the job in the development of the JHA. These are the steps involved in creating a JHA (Examples of JHA's can be found on your state OSHA Web site or at www.workplacesafetynow.com):

List all job steps or tasks that the worker must perform to complete the job. Create this list by watching the employee perform the operation in question, recording each step of the process, and reviewing the list with the employee for completeness.

Review each step to determine what safety and health hazards are or could be present; these should be listed as well. Further observation may be necessary to ensure all possible hazards are identified.

Determine what measures, if any, can eliminate or lessen the risk of injury or illness to the employee from the identified hazards. These measures can include: engineering controls, such as guarding or ventilation; work practices; administrative controls, such as job rotation; and PPE.

Perform initial hazard assessments prior to the introduction of new raw materials, equipment, or processes to the workplace and before major changes are made to processes, equipment, or the work environment. These assessments are made to ensure that employees will be protected from potential safety and health hazards.

Regardless of the technique used to identify hazards, all employees should know how to report workplace safety and health hazards in order to have them evaluated and corrected. Management should encourage use of the reporting system, and you should respond to complaints in a timely fashion. Update employees about the status of the complaint investigation and its outcome.

Some employers feel there is benefit in having someone from outside of the organization inspect or audit a facility's workplace safety program. This person may have more specialized knowledge in the safety and health field than others in the organization. An outsider may also recognize hazards you have overlooked. Sources for on-site help with occupational safety and health issues include consultants from governmental assistance offices, private firms, insurance company loss-control representatives, and occupational safety practitioners.

Hazard Resolution

After hazards are identified, they should be eliminated or abated to the degree that it is feasible. Both OSHA and best practices principles promote a hierarchy of control measures. At the top of the hierarchy are *engineering controls*, which include tactics such as machine guarding, guardrails, ventilation, and raw material substitution. All reasonably feasible engineering controls should be exhausted before other measures are taken.

Work practices, another technique for employee protection, involves modifying tasks and jobs to reduce employee exposure to hazards. These include measures such as wetting down areas to keep airborne dust levels to a minimum, or replacing lids on solvent degreasing tanks when not in use. Administrative controls, such as job rotation, are other tools employers sometimes use to reduce employee exposure.

Personal protective equipment (PPE), such as respirators, gloves, and safety glasses, should be used only as a last resort, after all feasible engineering and administrative controls and work practices have been implemented.

Employee input about abatement techniques is highly recommended. Employees may be able to provide insight regarding equipment and work procedures or have their own ideas about how to abate the hazards. They often are familiar with the history of the process and what measures have been tried in the past. Employees are also more likely to use the control measures and incorporate safe work practices if they feel some ownership in their development. Consider giving employees the authority and ability to correct hazards themselves whenever feasible.

Regular preventive maintenance of equipment is also important to prevent the occurrence of safety and health hazards. Examples of items that require regular inspection and maintenance include ladders, forklifts, hoists and slings, exhaust fans and belts, and pressure vessels. Some processing equipment may require a full mechanical integrity program with written inspection and testing procedures performed on a regular schedule. Proper housekeeping methods can also reduce health hazards by reducing airborne dust levels of hazardous substances and improving overall indoor air quality.

Once an organization has identified its existing and potential hazards, it's time to implement systems that prevent or resolve those hazards.

At the end of the day, whenever possible, hazards should be eliminated. Sometimes that can be done through substitution of a less toxic material or engineering controls. When hazards cannot be eliminated, systems should be established to control them. Some actions to consider are:

- Set up safe work procedures based on an analysis of the hazards at the workplace and ensure that employees understand and follow them. Involve employees in the analysis that results in those procedures.

- Be ready to enforce the rules for safe work procedures. Ask employees to help establish a disciplinary system that will be fair and understood by everyone.

- Where necessary, ensure that PPE is used and that employees know why they need it, how to use it, and how to maintain it.

- Provide for routine equipment maintenance to prevent breakdowns that can create hazards.

- Ensure that preventive and regular maintenance is tracked to completion.

- Plan for emergencies, including fire and natural disasters. Conduct frequent drills to ensure that all employees know what to do under stressful conditions.

Incident Investigation

Incident investigation (also known as accident investigation) is a key component of a safety and health program. The goal of an incident investigation should be hazard identification and prevention. It should not be to affix blame.

All events that cause injuries or property damage should be examined. When possible, all near misses (those events where injury or property damage does not occur, but could have if conditions were different) should also be investigated.

Incident investigations should be started as soon as possible. Precautions should be taken to control any remaining hazards in the area before the investigation begins.

OSHA programs describe three cause levels for incidents:

Direct causes. The immediate causes of the injury, illness, or damage. Direct causes are the hazardous material(s) or energy (e.g., electrical energy, potential energy, or heat) that caused the injury or damage.

Indirect causes. Unsafe actions and conditions that caused the hazardous materials or energy to exceed safe limits.

Basic causes. Those that contribute to the creation of the indirect hazards. These can include poor management policies, personal factors, or environmental factors.

Incident investigations should be a team effort, including supervision. And it's best to involve someone familiar with the process or equipment involved in the incident.

Incident investigations are used to identify the causes of incidents and to determine how to eliminate one or more of these causes to prevent other incidents.

Investigators need to ask questions, such as:

- Who was involved in the event?
- Who witnessed the event?
- What happened?
- What was abnormal or different before the incident occurred?
- When did each event in the incident occur?
- Where did the hazard first occur?
- How and why did an event take place?

The investigation process should include:

- Incident site examination
- Witness interviews
- Documentation (including notes, maps, sketches, and photographs)
- Review of operating procedures

- Process information (i.e., flow charts, chemical properties, equipment diagrams, and normal operating limits), maintenance records, and job hazard analyses
- Development of a sequence of events leading up to the incident

Each contributing factor should be traced back to its root cause. A written report (see Selected References and Resources, "Manager/Supervisor Incident Investigation Report Example") that describes the incident, its causes, and recommendations for corrective action and prevention should be prepared.

Emergency response to the incident should also be reviewed. Among the factors to be considered are whether each employee responded to the emergency situation appropriately, whether first aid was administered to sick or injured employees in an adequate and timely manner, and whether the emergency response team's PPE and other necessary equipment was available in a usable condition for immediate use during the emergency.

The ultimate goal of the investigation is to determine the basic and root causes of the incident and to determine appropriate corrective action so that it does not happen again. Simply attributing an incident to "employee error," without further consideration of the basic causes, deprives the organization of the opportunity to take real preventive action. Engineering controls, improved work practices, and administrative controls should be considered to help employees do their jobs safely. Your management practices should also be considered as a possible factor. If there is managerial or supervisory pressure to increase production or cut costs, employees may take unsafe shortcuts in work procedures, or necessary preventive maintenance may be delayed or skipped.

Injury and Illness Care and Treatment

It's imperative that leaders and managers work with their workers' compensation carrier and insurance agent or broker to help develop an occupational medical program that fits the organization's workplace. This is discussed in detail in Chapter 5. Here are a few key points:

- Get to know the best workers' compensation doctors in the area. Not only should they be medically qualified, they should understand the nuances of the workers' compensation system.

- Directly pay for occupational ("first-aid") cases when doing so is financially and regulatorily appropriate. Ask your insurance agent or other professional to conduct an analysis to best determine a course of action.

- Involve nearby doctors and emergency facilities by inviting them to visit the workplace and help plan the best way to treat employees in case of injury or illness.

- Ensure the available access of medical personnel to provide advice and consultation on matters of employee health. (This does not mean that you/your company provide expert advice on healthcare; however, you must be prepared to deal with medical emergencies or health problems connected to your workplace.)

To fulfill these requirements, consider these steps:

- Develop an emergency medical procedure to handle injuries, transport ill or injured workers, and notify medical facilities. Don't let injured workers drive to the doctor; have a supervisor take them or drive them yourself.

- Post emergency numbers.

- Survey the medical facilities near your place of business and make arrangements for them to handle routine and emergency cases. (Cooperative agreements may be possible with nearby larger workplaces that have on-site medical personnel and/or facilities.)

- Consider connecting with a local doctor or an occupational health nurse on an as-needed basis for advice on medical and first-aid planning.

- Ensure that your procedure for reporting injuries and illnesses is understood by all employees.

- If your business is remote (including construction work sites) from medical facilities, you are required to ensure that adequately trained personnel are available to render first aid. First-aid supplies must be readily available for emergency use. Arrangements for this training can be made through your local safety council (American Association of Safety Councils or National Safety Council), Red Cross chapter, workers' compensation insurance carrier, and others.

TRAINING AND EDUCATION

An effective workplace safety program requires proper job safety performance from everyone in the workplace. Leaders and managers must ensure that all employees know about the materials and equipment they use, known hazards, and how to resolve/control the hazards. Each employee needs to know that:

- No employee is expected to undertake a job until she has received job instructions on how to do it properly and is authorized to perform that job.
- No employee should undertake a job that appears unsafe.
- You have trained your employees on every potential hazard that they could be exposed to and how to protect themselves.

You may be able to combine safety and health training with other training, depending on the types of hazards in your workplace.

It's imperative that employees *really understand* the information being taught. Pay particular attention to your new employees and to employees who are moving to new jobs. Train your supervisors to understand all the hazards faced by the employees and how to reinforce training with quick reminders and refreshers, or with disciplinary action if necessary. And as we discussed at the beginning of this chapter, you must communicate safety to your employees in a language they understand.

A written workplace safety program is just words on paper if you, your supervisors, and employees are not aware of it and don't understand it. Observing employees' understanding of safe practices is a more efficient measure than employees simply telling you or saying that they understand.

Employees cannot follow safety rules, identify hazards, use correct work procedures or protective equipment, or work to achieve goals if they do not have the necessary knowledge to do so. Furthermore, if employees are afraid to discuss safety and health concerns with management or have no clear method of reporting their concerns to management, safety and health hazards can go undetected. Uncorrected hazards can adversely affect employee morale and productivity, even if an incident, injury, or illness does not occur as a result.

While communication regarding safety and health issues should be a continual process, there are times when it is especially critical, including:

- The beginning of an employee's new job assignment
- Whenever material, process, or procedural changes are implemented
- Whenever the employer notices deficiencies in safe work practices

Communication

Safety training should go beyond the minimum requirements set by OSHA regulations. Some key points when incorporating training are:

- Engage employees directly into the training delivery by using pictures, video, and multimedia (involving employees) to make them part of the process. It's okay to use generic/core training materials; however, make them personal to your work environment for the best affect.
- Supervisors should receive at least as much safety and health training as front-line employees, if not more.
- The design of a training session should be based on clearly stated goals and objectives. The goals and objectives should reflect the knowledge and skills employees need to do their jobs safely and should be as specific as possible.
- Training content should be directly applicable to the hazards, procedures, and equipment the employees encounter on the job.
- Employees are more receptive to training if they see *how* they can apply the training to their work.
- Training content must cover emergency procedures as well as normal day-to-day activities.
- Because individuals learn in different ways, the variety of training methods should be used to help communicate the material to be learned. You will read in Chapter 7 that changing an employee's role (having him or her conduct training) will positively and forever change his/her safety behavior.
- Some trainers develop games to review material, especially for refresher training.

- There should also be some way to check for employee understanding of the course content to ensure transfer of the training to the workplace. Methods often used include class discussion, written tests and quizzes, demonstrations, and on-the-job observations.

- Supervisors can lead the majority of safety training sessions; however, it's imperative that front-line employees also lead safety meetings.

- Supervisors can observe and coach their employees by correcting unsafe work practices as they occur and positively reinforcing the use of safe work practices.

- Employees can be encouraged to work with each other to reinforce workplace safety. This is especially important when more experienced employees work with new employees.

- Experienced employees should teach newer employees safe work practices rather than risky shortcuts.

- Other methods of communicating job safety and health information include posters, employee handbooks, and handout materials, including one-page fact sheets or booklets, computer-based learning, and safety promotional activities.

- If posters are used, they should have a clear message and be located in areas where employees are likely to see them, such as near the time clock or in the cafeteria. *It's highly recommended that you incorporate your employees (think of how Wal-Mart incorporates their Associates in print ads) in the posters rather than using generic "be safe" posters. With the availability of digital cameras and a color printer, it's a small investment with a big payoff.* Posters should be rotated regularly.

- Relying on written materials only can be ineffective for several reasons:

  - Many working adults may lack basic reading skills. To avoid embarrassment and humiliation, they will often hide this from their supervisors and coworkers. Due to the growing diversity of today's workforce, many workers have limited English speaking and reading skills.

  - It is also common for a person to set aside reading material "for later, when I have time" and never pick it up again. These problems can be addressed at least partially by having the employees complete worksheets or quizzes about the written material and submit them to their supervisor or the safety coordinator for grading.

- Increasing numbers of businesses are turning to computer-based learning as a training method. Computer-based learning can combine video, sound, and text in an interactive format that can test employees for completion and understanding. Several standardized programs are available in this format, and many employers are developing their own.

- Safety promotional activities, such as fairs, dinners, and safety standdowns, can also be an effective method of communicating the importance of workplace safety to employees. Employers must be careful, however, that "incentive programs" do not send the wrong message. For example, some programs (based on the number or frequency of lost-time injuries) have resulted in the underreporting of injuries by employees. (See Chapter 7 for an expanded discussion on this subject.)

- One of the strongest methods of communication is by example. Managers and supervisors must model their actions for employees by working safely and following all safety and health rules.

Effective communication flows in two directions. Employees must feel free to discuss their safety concerns with their supervisors without fear of retaliation. They should know the proper procedures for reporting safety and health hazards in the workplace to get the hazards corrected or to get their questions answered. Supervisors should know whom to contact for assistance in addressing safety issues and have the authority to take appropriate corrective action. You should work to ensure that communication is occurring on all levels of the organization.

RECORDKEEPING

Document your activities in all elements of your workplace safety program. Essential records, including those legally required for workers' compensation, insurance audits, and government inspections, must be maintained as long as the actual need exists or as required by law. Keeping records of your activities, such as policy statements, training sessions, safety and health meetings, information distributed to employees, and medical arrangements made, is greatly encouraged.

Maintaining essential records also will demonstrate sound business management as supporting proof for credit applications, for showing "good faith" in reducing any proposed penalties from OSHA inspections, and for insurance and other audits. Good records also will aid efficient review of your current safety and health activities for better control of your operations and to plan improvements.

Records of sales, costs, profits, and losses are essential to all successful businesses. They enable the owner or manager to learn from experience and to make corrections for future operations. Records of incidents, related injuries, illnesses, and property losses can serve the same purpose, if they are used in the same way. The primary purpose of OSHA-required recordkeeping is to retain information about incidents that have happened to help determine the causes and develop procedures to prevent recurrences.

Injury and Illness Records

OSHA rules for recording and reporting occupational injuries and illnesses affect 1.4 million establishments. Small businesses with 10 or fewer employees throughout the year may be exempt from most of the requirements of the OSHA recordkeeping rules. And some industries, such as service, finance, insurance, and real estate, may be exempt or classified as low hazard. Detailed information about OSHA recordkeeping rules can be found at www.osha.gov/recordkeeping/index.html.

The OSHA recordkeeping system has five steps:

Obtain a report on every injury or job-related illness requiring medical treatment (other than basic first aid).

Record each injury or job-related illness on OSHA Form 300 (Log of Work-Related Injuries and Illnesses).

Prepare a supplementary record of occupational injuries and illnesses for recordable cases on OSHA Form 301 (Injuries and Illnesses Incident Report). However, in most states, the workers' compensation report of injury form is sufficient, so OSHA Form 301 does not have to be completed separately.

Report to OSHA within eight hours of a serious incident, all work-related fatalities or multiple hospitalizations that involve three or more employees.

Even if a business is exempt from routine recordkeeping requirements, it may be selected by the Federal Bureau of Labor Statistics (BLS) or a related state agency for inclusion in an annual sample survey. You will receive a letter directly from the agency with instructions, if you are selected.

In addition:

- Every year, prepare an annual summary using OSHA Form 300A (Summary of Work-Related Injuries and Illnesses). Post it no later than February 1, and keep it posted until May 1. A good place to post it is next to the OSHA Workplace Poster.
- Retain these records for at least five years.
- Periodically review these records to look for any patterns or repeat situations. These records identify an organization's high-risk areas that may require immediate attention.

Basic OSHA recordkeeping requirements address only injuries and illnesses; many organizations expand their records to include all incidents, including those where no injury or illness resulted, such as near misses. This information can help pinpoint unsafe actions, conditions, and/or procedures.

Safety councils, insurance carriers, private consultants, and others can assist you in instituting such a recordkeeping system.

Exposure Records and Others

In addition to injury and illness records, certain OSHA standards require records on the exposure of employees to toxic substances and hazardous exposures, physical examination reports, inspection records, safety committee meeting minutes, safety training records, and employment records. As you identify hazards and hazard resolution steps, you will be able to determine whether these requirements apply to your workplace. Your records should be used in conjunction with your control procedures and with your self-inspection activity. They should not be considered merely as bookkeeping.

BEST PRACTICES

A safe and healthful workplace depends on effective management to ensure that hazards are identified and that effective physical and administrative protections are established and maintained.

Business owners and managers need to recognize that their role is essential to the establishment and implementation of an effective safety and health program. Owners and managers must:

- Establish and communicate policies
- Guide their subordinates to set safety and health goals and objectives
- Provide needed resources including money, machines, materials, methods, staffing and time; and they must motivate personnel through active participation in and support of safety and health activities

Earlier we covered core regulatory items for the development of your workplace safety program. Keeping within the OSHA core elements structure, we have expanded/summarized to include some additional best practices:

- Identify safety as a company value (see Chapter 7).
- Emphasize management commitment and responsibility (via the assignment of safety and health authority and responsibility to supervisors and employees; and a system to hold them accountable).

  - Draft a company policy regarding safety and health, and make it available to all employees. A policy statement from top management would help to inform your employees of the strength of management's commitment to workplace safety and health.
  - Establish clear goals and objectives regarding employee safety and health, and communicate these goals and objectives to all personnel, from upper-level supervisors to those personnel performing specific job tasks.
  - Recognize the *economic* and *social value* of a commitment to workplace safety and health, and then visibly demonstrate that commitment through appropriate leadership, participation, and support (top management).

- Consistently practice safe and healthful work habits, and show genuine concern about identifying and controlling hazards. Set an example for employees, and eliminate a common excuse employees use for ignoring safe and healthful practices.
- Provide those personnel to whom you have assigned authority and responsibility with necessary resources, in money, time, and staffing, to effectively accomplish established objectives.
- Conduct constructive performance appraisals relating to the safe performance of their job activities in order to ensure that personnel at all levels are performing in the manner prescribed.
- Establish policies and mechanisms to periodically evaluate the safety and effectiveness of your safety and health program, note deficiencies, make recommendations for improvement, and implement needed changes. In some companies, such a review is commonly a function of a safety committee, equally represented by both management and employees.

- Involve employees.

  - Encourage employees to participate in safety and health activities by providing systems for employee input and assistance in identifying and resolving safety and health problems. (Such systems might include safety committees, safety suggestions systems, promotion programs, and quality circles.)
  - Clearly define the safety and health responsibilities of all personnel, and communicate these responsibilities through formal policies, procedures, rules, and training. Managers, supervisors, and employees in all parts of the organization need to know what is expected of them.

- Perform work-site analysis.

  - Have an expert in safety and health conduct periodic work-site audits to assist in identifying hazards, to verify the adequacy of existing hazard controls, and to help you keep current with changing safety and health requirements.
  - Conduct routine analysis of planned changes in production, processing, facilities, and materials to help you to anticipate and deal

effectively with any safety- and health-related effects arising from such changes.

- Define processes, procedures, and activities that present known hazards. Where risk is the greatest, conduct a job or task hazard analysis to establish effective procedures for eliminating or controlling the hazards defined. A review of the steps involved in each of your work-site jobs can identify hazards or potential hazards. These reviews will enable you to anticipate and prevent injuries and illnesses rather than react to them after they occur.

- To detect recurring hazards, previously missed hazards, and failures in hazard control, conduct frequent self-inspections of the facility or work site using staff personnel who have received training in basic hazard recognition.

- Establish systems and mechanisms that enable employees to report potentially hazardous conditions to management. These should include follow-up and feedback to ensure that employee concerns for safety and health are effectively addressed.

- Formally review all incidents and near-miss incidents to help determine what caused them to happen and to prevent their recurrence.

- Conduct a review of your injury and illness experience using documents such as OSHA Form 300, incident reports, and first-aid reports. Use these tools to detect patterns that might indicate a need for you to take corrective or preventive action.

- Implement hazard recognition and resolution procedures.

  - Establish and implement specific formal policies, procedures, rules, and methods to ensure the application of engineering controls, administrative controls, and the appropriate use of PPE to prevent and control hazards. In addition to general safety and health rules and discipline, typical policies and procedures might include: lock-out/tag-out, hazard communication, emergency planning, hearing conservation, process safety management, respirator use and care, materials handling, tool safety, machine guarding, or others suited to your work-site operations and activities.

  - Establish engineering and maintenance systems, programs, and policies to ensure that all equipment, tools, and machines (including PPE) are safely maintained in accordance with manufacturer recommendations.

- Review work processes to identify potential emergencies, then develop a plan for responding to them, to allow quick reaction to prevent serious harm. Train personnel on the emergency plan, and conduct drills where appropriate to ensure that supervisors and employees know immediately what to do if an emergency arises.

- Conspicuously post emergency telephone numbers and other emergency information, and identify exits and emergency exit routes to strengthen the ability for quick and safe response to emergencies.

- Where appropriate, obtain the assistance of occupational safety professionals to identify health-related hazards and to help train employees to recognize, prevent, and control such exposures. Types of assistance are: noise abatement, hazardous materials exposure abatement, ergonomics evaluation, ventilation design, respiratory protection methods, process safety management, and so forth.

- Where an infirmary, clinic, hospital, or physician is not reasonably accessible in terms of time or distance for the treatment of all injured employees, provide suitable first-aid supplies at a readily available location to assist in emergency care, and ensure that an adequately trained person is available to render first aid.

- Institute training and education (of supervisors and employees about the hazards they are exposed to, and the control of those hazards).

  - Provide formal and informal training, including on-the-job training, to help employees recognize, protect against, and control the specific hazard exposures relating to their job activities. Educating employees of the hazards of their work, how they can be hurt, the nature of the potential harm, and how to work safely will increase the likelihood that they will work safely. Reinforcing workers' safe practices by acknowledging employees, and by providing retraining or discipline for unsafe work, will ensure that they know you are committed to their safety and health.

  - Ensure that the employees who supervise others follow safety and health rules and safe work practices. Supervisors need to be instructed in their responsibilities and the reasons for those responsibilities. In addition, supervisors should receive training in work-site hazard analysis. Such training teaches employees to recognize the hazards in jobs under their supervision and to understand how the hazards can cause harm and the nature of that harm. They learn to develop appropriate rules and work practices necessary for control of workplace hazards. Supervisors also need training on how to educate their staff in safe and healthful work practices and on how to enforce those practices.

- Institute recordkeeping.

CHAPTER 4

Critical Safety Considerations: Focusing Workplace Safety Efforts

In Chapter 1 we discussed the critical strategic and tactical elements workplace safety programs contain. Developing a workplace safety program is strategic, while identifying a particular hazard and implementing controls to reduce the potential for it to result in an injury or illness is tactical. Tactical activities, again focused on reducing injuries and illnesses, are best recognized through the reduction of unsafe acts and conditions.

TAKING A LOOK BACK

The best place for these strategic and tactical activities to be found is in your workplace safety programs. In Chapter 3 we highlighted program development, structure, components and best practices. Here it is essential to ask yourself if the plan that you have or will be developing considers critical safety considerations—that is, hazards found within your operations. If after looking at the list of potential safety considerations that should be represented in your program, you're satisfied with the depth and capabilities, then you've done a fine job. If you recognize that additional detail and hazard control activities, such as training and personal protective equipment (PPE), need to be considered, then adjustments, large or small, should be made to your workplace safety program. This chapter will help you with that backward look and whatever refinements your program may need.

Literature in the safety arena suggests that the vast majority of injuries and illness at work occur due to unsafe acts, not conditions. This distinction makes sense if we look at how work is accomplished today as opposed to the 1960s, for instance. As service industries have overtaken manufacturing, the conditional aspect (e.g., unsafe conditions) of work produces fewer injuries than do unsafe acts. This distinction is essential as you look to not only what hazards might exist within your firm's operations, but what hazards actually exist. The distinction can be made for what employees "do" and to hazards from the use of tools, equipment, and processes employed. Further, understanding the distinction between unsafe acts and unsafe conditions makes Chapter 2 much more relevant. In developing hazard assessment tools, such as checklists, you must be capable of integrating considerations from both perspectives. Hazards must be recognized as well as where they emanate from.

Earlier we asked that you consider the identified hazards (the assessments in Chapter 2) and develop a workplace safety program (as suggested in Chapter 3). Workplace safety programs must avoid the critical trap of being too general. Your workplace safety program must be capable of identifying and responding to—that is, eliminating or controlling—general and specific hazards. This chapter helps you focus on some of the specific hazards that exist in the working world. It is impossible for us to provide an overview of all of the specific hazards that exist in industry. However, if your hazard analysis is sufficiently robust, you'll be able to identify specific hazards. Then you can implement control methods and deploy proper training.

Technology, the speed of information, and the skills that workers bring to an employer have dramatically changed the hazards to which workers are exposed. What businesses are experiencing today with the types and speed of equipment is analogous to the industrial revolution of the nineteenth century. Expanded capabilities not only create new expectations, they result in new occupational hazards. For some, the changes are exciting; for others, changes result in stress and pressure on the job. Modern technologies, of course, create new hazards that we must be aware of and despite technological advancements, the working world remains filled with injury and illness exposures.

Hazards, whether developing, new, or those that have existed for some time, must be recognized. A safety and health practitioner should be able to:

- Distinguish hazards that will develop based on projected changes in operations, new technologies, and materials being considered.
- Recognize, as quickly as possible, new hazards in the workplace.
- Retain knowledge on existing hazards and continuing efforts to control them.

Ensuring that you can project possible future hazards, recognize new ones, and manage those that exist takes practice and involvement. It is critical, for example, that departments such as purchasing, facilities, engineering, warehousing, planning, and finance let the individual in charge of safety and health in on their future plans. As the owner (and safety and health manager), you should not be the last to know that new chemicals are being introduced or that engineering is installing the latest and greatest overhead crane. Nor should you be the last to know that business acquisitions are being considered or that new locations are being looked at.

Without knowing as early as possible about new operations, projected changes, equipment upgrades, and the like, you (and in larger companies the human resources professional, plant manager, or company vice president managing safety) will face many challenges in controlling hazards.

As an owner and manager, you play a critical role in determining and developing, new, and existing hazards and controlling them. More important though, is the fact that you individual understand that the hazards are not and will not all be general in nature. Many will be very specific, requiring specific analysis and controls.

CRITICAL CONNECTIONS: SAFETY AND SPECIAL HAZARDS

The best way to expand on the importance of specific or special hazards in the workplace is to highlight many that often exist and to use them as *exemplars*. Those hazards are valuable to understand for at least two reasons.

First, they play a vital role in an individual responsible for safety and health's skill development in what to look for in the future (hazard identification). Second, recognizing the hazards helps to become better at assuring your company is focused upon regulatory compliance.

Think of the advantages of developing a training program before employees are actually exposed to a hazard. To say the least, that scenario would be unique for most businesses. Business and operational corollaries abound, however. Buildings are not constructed without blueprints; why should an operation begin before training takes place? Think of the training efforts, then, as a blueprint page to control unsafe acts and conditions. The blueprint analogy is especially important when faced with special or unique hazards in the workplace. General training does not work; training must be specific to the hazards.

A list of special or specific hazards is provided later in this chapter. Some you will recognize, others you will not. Further, many represent those your employees will never be exposed to due to the nature of your operations. We mention these only to suggest that the hazards you must identify might be quite varied.

By highlighting specific hazards, we'll be able to show not only the importance of identification and control, but the importance of recognizing them so that you can make them part of your workplace safety program efforts. Of course, these efforts include ensuring your safety assessments are capable of identifying such special or specific hazards, that your safety program integrates them, that training is focused, and that appropriate personal protective equipment is provided, where required.

Before we discuss the exemplars, we'd like to highlight a few of the universal benefits to truly understanding as many of the hazards within your operations as possible. Such reviews benefit program development in at least five ways, including:

- Enhancing your knowledge of a particular hazard (i.e., enhancing your skills in determining how critical a particular hazard may be)
- Improving your overall hazard recognition skills
- Understanding control measures specific to the operations and workplace hazards focused on those operations
- Creating relevant training programs
- Complying with applicable state, federal, and/or local regulations

Once again, we stress that it is important to understand specific or special hazards; all hazards your organization will face are not general in nature. If hazards are not general, then general controls will not be sufficient to control them. Therefore, you may need to adopt special or specific controls and safeguards. In addition, specific regulatory mandates likely apply. Visualize our discussion as a closed loop (see Exhibit 4.1).

In the operational assessment, the person or position responsible for workplace safety becomes familiar with operations, preferably in detail. Once operations are understood, a hazard assessment can be undertaken. This assessment determines whether the hazards identified are general in nature or are specific. Once the hazards are known, physical, administrative, and training controls can be implemented. Training is listed separately, as it is vital to determine if the training can be general or if the specific hazards identified may require prescribed training activities. Subsequent to all of the analyses, a review of applicable regulations can be conducted to ascertain compliance. Where compliance may be in question, modifications or enhancements can then be made to hazard identification activities, controls, training programs, and your organization's written workplace safety program.

This process is a closed loop—you must continue to cycle through the analysis, improvement, training, and compliance process. It really never ends. Changes in personnel, operations, laws, and so forth will all be triggers to keep this activity alive. In fact, you can conduct the regulatory review twice, once at the beginning of the assessment to establish a baseline and then again after enhancements have been instituted, to validate your compliance efforts minimally meet legal/regulatory demands.

EXHIBIT 4.1   CLOSED LOOP ANALYSIS AND PROGRAM DEVELOPMENT

Regulatory Compliance Overview
↓

Operational → Hazard → Controls → Training → Regulatory
Assessment   Assessment   and Programs   Compliance
                                                      Overview

SPECIFIC HAZARDS REVIEW

Let's review several specific industries and hazards. We have chosen these examples for two reasons:

Specific controls are required to manage hazards associated with operations.

Specific regulations (usually) apply that those responsible for workplace safety must be cognizant of.

Each of the hazards to be discussed has specific hazard(s) and control considerations as well as regulatory compliance demands. As you review these, keep the closed loop analysis discussion in mind. Such a review is important for activities, for example, within construction operations. Hazards can change frequently, even throughout the day; thus, hazard assessment capabilities must be continuous.

Construction Safety: Specific Hazards Example 1

Those companies that make their living in the construction business usually understand the need for identifying job site hazards and the controls necessary for related exposures to their employees. However, many businesses that have to comply with general industry safety orders (i.e., Fed/OSHA CFR (Code of Federal Regulations) 1910 et seq.) may need to comply with some construction safety orders as well (e.g., Fed/OSHA CFR 1926). Many organizations that do their own facility repairs, using special tools and construction processes, have to comply with such orders.

To control hazards specific to construction operations, the appropriate hazard recognition activities must be in place and regulatory requirements must be understood. The use of general industry safety orders will not suffice for most construction hazards. There are, however, general industry safety orders that apply to construction operations. Confusing? No. General industry safety orders apply to all businesses for those hazards that are present, but specific regulations or safety orders may not apply to businesses that otherwise need to comply with the general industry safety orders. It is incumbent on you (or in larger organizations, the safety and health manager) to recognize the difference in compliance requirements. He or she can do this only if he understands and identifies actual hazards.

As you might suspect, construction operations can create numerous injury exposures: falls, trenching and shoring, the need for personal protective gear, and many others.

Bloodborne Pathogens and Other Biological Exposures: Specific Hazard Example 2

Exposure to bloodborne pathogens (BBP) exists in all industries, not just healthcare and public service. For example, any organization that provides first-aid or emergency assistance to employees or the public may have exposures to BBP and need to adopt appropriate controls.

Controls for BBPs are based on the assumption that anyone can have been exposed and become or may be infected by BBPs, whether HIV or Hepatitis B or C. Because we may never know who has been exposed, controls are found within what are referred to as universal controls. In addition, controls focus on OPIMs (other potentially infectious materials). OPIMs might include, for example, bedding, clothing, bandaging materials, needles, and so on (anything that serves as a potential transfer medium for infected substances, such as bodily fluids).

Understanding BBP controls and complying with applicable regulations demands at a minimum that you understand:

- Requirements for engineering and work practices, those who are allowed and those who are excluded from handling infectious materials or OPIMs
- Handling and disposing of "sharps"—needles and other medical devices and equipment
- Handling, labeling, and disposing of waste or OPIMs
- Cleaning and decontaminating equipment, surfaces, and the work site after an event where infectious fluids or materials may be present
- Availability and use of PPE
- Personal hygiene and laundry

We need to reiterate a couple of important points here. Bloodborne pathogen exposures may come from many different sources. It is incumbent upon the employer to know what those exposures are and to ascertain that employees are taking appropriate steps to control the exposures. As mentioned, bloodborne pathogens exposure is not limited to the health-care environment or the public safety arena. If you have employees who might provide first aid or respond to a medical emergency, your program must recognize these exposures and implement the proper controls.

There are many other BBP control considerations, and a wide variety of materials are available to help you understand them. Sites such as Fed/OSHA's (www.osha.gov), Cal/OSHA's (www.dir.ca.gov/dosh) as well as the Centers for Disease Control and Prevention (www.cdc.gov), and many others will be helpful.

Ergonomics: Specific Hazard Example 3

National Overview

Two of OSHA's 26 state occupational safety and health programs—California and Washington—have adopted state ergonomics standards. The Washington ergonomics standard was subsequently repealed in 2003. Employers in California are required to comply with the specific provisions of the state's ergonomics standard. The discussion that follows provides some examples of state plan ergonomics efforts.

California adopted an ergonomics standard on November 14, 1996 (see www.dir.ca.gov/title8/5110.html). The standard provides that when at least two employees performing identical tasks have been diagnosed by a physician with repetitive motion injuries (RMIs) within 12 consecutive months, the employer must establish a program that shall:

- Evaluate each job, process, or operation of identical activity for exposures which have caused RMIs at the affected work site.
- Control or minimize to the extent feasible the exposures that have caused repetitive motion injuries, considering engineering controls and administrative controls.
- Provide training to affected employees.

California OSHA is conducting inspections as well as outreach activities and has developed publications and training materials concerning ergonomics (available at www.dir.ca.gov/dosh/puborder.asp).

Washington adopted an ergonomics standard on May 26, 2000, but it was repealed December 2003. With the repeal, Washington is concentrating on educating workers and employers on the importance of preventing ergonomic injuries and proper techniques they can use. Enforcement issues are currently being addressed on a case-by-case basis.

Alaska held public meetings statewide in January 2002 on a draft standard for general safety and health programs, which included ergonomics; however, due to the number of comments received, the Commissioner of Labor decided to drop the ergonomics provisions and later discontinued efforts to develop a safety and health programs rule.

Minnesota has established an Ergonomics Task Force to recommend approaches the state can take to reduce work-related musculoskeletal disorders. (For more information on this task force, see www.doli.state.mn .us/ergo.html.)

Oregon's OSHA strategic plan includes activities designed to reduce musculoskeletal injuries through outreach and the use of voluntary services. (For more information see www.cbs.state.or.us/external/osha/ subjects/com%2001%20ergonomic.html.) Oregon has also created an ergonomics stakeholder group to identify strategies to promote reduction of ergonomic injuries in targeted industries with high rates of musculoskeletal injuries. In addition, Oregon's OSHA offers a variety of ergonomics-related services including conferences, on-site training, educational resources, and consultation services to help Oregon employers.

Ergonomics at Your Company

Many people get work-related back injuries, wrist disorders, and assorted strains and sprains. The injuries may occur suddenly or may develop slowly over time. Sometimes improving the fit between employees and their work can help prevent these injuries; however, often away-from-work factors complicate the ergonomics process.

We can't do the subject of ergonomics justice in the few paragraphs we have allocated, so we encourage you to refer to the links provided and to visit the Sample References and Resources section of this book. We also encourage you to be open to new ways of thinking about ergonomics, such as reading landmark works by Kate Montgomery and Anthony Carey.[1] Each brings a unique approach to ergonomics not practiced among most safety practitioners today.

In straightforward ergonomics, fitting the task to the person means adjusting the way in which work is done; modifying equipment, job design, and layout; and adjusting for the physical capabilities of workers so that work does not cause musculoskeletal disorders. Some basic ergonomic adjustments include:

- Moving things in closer and within easy reach
- Raising or lowering chair or work surface
- Building in adjustability and redesign work areas for a comfortable work position
- Using the right tool for the task
- Being flexible and modifying your expectations according to employees' size and strength
- Providing adjustable equipment and workstations to accommodate differences in employee size
- Using tools with handles that fit comfortably in the hands of your employees—this allows them to work in a comfortable position (e.g., using vertical handles to accommodate different heights)
- Reducing force and repetition by using power tools (when appropriate)
- Trying to redesign tasks that require repeated, forceful hand and tool use

In addition:

- When possible, have employees put the work in front of them at about waist height.
- Teach everyone the importance of smart lifting:
  - Use a hand truck or to get help with large loads.
  - Avoid bending and twisting the back when lifting.
  - Bend at the knees and keep back straight to lift loads from the floor.
  - *Lift like a baby.* (Watch two-year-olds lift something off the floor: They use perfect posture, squatting down using the strength of their legs to balance and lift.)
  - Try to design work so that loads are lighter, heavy loads are stored at waist height, and less lifting is required.

- Change the size or weight of the load to accommodate differences in strength.

More than 2,000 studies on musculoskeletal disorders (MSDs) have been conducted by the Centers for Disease Control and Prevention (CDC) and the National Institute for Occupational Safety and Health (NIOSH).[2] In addition to making environmental changes (at home and on the job), the findings indicate that exercising, stretching, and physical balance are critical components to minimizing the potential for musculoskeletal disorders. Based on the research, circumstances that lead to musculoskeletal disorders are most likely multiple in origin.

It's important to note that NIOSH and the CDC have also identified individual (personal) factors associated with work-related musculoskeletal disorders (MSDs). The relationship of these individual factors and the resulting risk of injury to an individual are complex and not yet fully understood. Among these factors are:

- *Gender.* Some studies have found a higher prevalence of some MSDs in women.

- *Cigarette smoking.* Some studies have found smoking related to pain in the extremities, including the neck and back. One hypothesis is that there is nicotine-induced diminished blood flow to vulnerable tissues.

- *Physical activity.* A lack (or overexertion) of physical activity may increase susceptibility to injury.

- *Strength.* The risk for musculoskeletal injuries (in some studies) was three times greater in weaker subjects.

- *Anthropometry.* Weight, height, body mass index (BMI) (a ratio of weight to height squared), and obesity all can play a role in MSD potential, especially carpal tunnel syndrome and lumbar disc herniation.

In a number of musculoskeletal injury cases, basic ergonomic changes alone will have minimal impact on the final outcome of an individual's health and recovery for two reasons. First, as shown in Exhibit 4.2, and based on 168 hours (7 days × 24 hours), activities at work constitute about 24 percent of an employees' life activities (based on a 40-hour workweek),

EXHIBIT 4.2   REAL TIME ON THE JOB
VERSUS OFF THE JOB

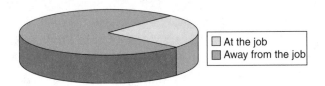

☐ At the job
■ Away from the job

and second, the best success seems to come from continuing to incorporate personal exercise, stretch activities, and functional posture at home and at work. As time away from the job constitutes so much of employees' life activities, obviously it is vital to examine away-from-work ergonomic/fitness activities.

Trenching and Excavation Work: Specific Hazard Example 4

For the most part, trenching and excavation work is performed by specialists, usually found in the construction industry. These firms tend to be knowledgeable about injury and illness exposures, safeguards, permit requirements, and the expanded hazards associated with trench and excavation work. By *expanded hazards* we are referring to the fact that a trench that is dug may require shoring to comply with necessary regulations and, more important, to maintain the health and safety of workers. Based on the characteristics of the trench, a comprehensive confined spaces program may be in order as well. As you might suspect, the actual hazards present may expand in severity potential and number; thus, regulatory compliance will expand as well.

For example, most of us recognize that trenches can collapse, trapping, crushing, and/or suffocating workers. Such incidents happen all too frequently. Unfortunately, hazards and controls for trenching are not restricted to collapses. Depending on the nature of the trench, it may have an atmosphere that is oxygen depleted or contaminated with toxic vapors. Or vapors present may be flammable. All of these traits turn a trench into a permit-required confined space. Additional regulations, safeguards, and training must be deployed based on the expanded, specific hazards.

Trenches of certain depths and in certain types of soil may require more than shoring; dewatering may be required, which is yet another consideration for the safety and health practitioner. Actually, the discussion of trench hazards is a very apt description of hazard expansion and mutation. In this case, what starts out as a trench in the soil can easily become a situation that is immediately dangerous to life and health (IDLH) from more than one hazard. Controls for these hazards may be found within several safety standards, both within the construction and in general industry arenas. (Other standards may apply based on where the operations are taking place and in what industry.)

Control of Hazardous Energy: Specific Hazard Example 5

Many refer to the control of hazardous energy as lock-out/block-out or lock-out/tag-out. Both of these terms refer to methods of controlling hazardous energy and are generally acceptable as catchall terms. However, from our experience, their use is mostly directed at electrical energy hazards. The benefits of using "control of hazardous energy" as the reference to the broadened source(s) of hazards and their controls are intentional. Besides electrical, several sources of energy need to be recognized and managed, including gravitational, mechanical, hydraulic, radiological, and pneumatic.

Commonalties exist among all of the sources of energy. As an example, their source not only needs to be controlled, but in many cases residual energy must be dissipated, or hazards will still exist. The power to a machine can be disconnected and that source locked out, but energy may still be stored in a capacitor—enough to cause serious harm or death. This residual energy must be "bled off," just like the residual compressed air in a tank, after the compressor has been turned off.

Understanding the source of energy is essential to establishing controls, developing safe work practices, complying with regulations, conducting adequate training, and providing appropriate personal protective equipment. Hazardous energy is an example of a specific safety hazard that requires specific controls. Regulatory mandates for these controls can be found within several safety standards or orders.

Respiratory Protection: Specific Hazard Example 6

Respiratory protection can take several forms: nuisance dust, vapor, or mist cartridges, full- or half-face masks, air purifying, or supplied air, for example. They all refer to various controls and, in most cases, carry with them specific regulatory mandates. Due to the specificity in the hazards—all respiratory hazards (and thus controls) are not the same—you must be able to distinguish among the many exposures or controls and determine which will be appropriate. For example, is a worker exposed to:

- An oxygen-deficient atmosphere?
- A hazardous atmosphere, such as one that is flammable?
- Atmospheres with only nuisance dusts, or IDLH environments?

Even if the proper respiratory selection has been made, training, conducted at the proper time by appropriate individuals, has to be brought into the mix. Other considerations apply as well. For example:

- Respirator maintenance
- Storage
- Fit testing
- Medical evaluations (required in many exposure cases even before an employee embarks on a task) to check fitness for duty

Consider also that, based on the capabilities of employees, air-supplied or powered air-purifying respirators may be necessary. The only way to recognize these needs is to:

- Understand the hazards.
- Recognize the hazards as special hazards.
- Provide the appropriate protection and safe work practices.

As with most all safety and health issues, respiratory protection is not one to mess around with. The potential for a significant impact on life and health is too great.

Motor Fleet and Vehicle Safety: Specific Hazard Example 7

We remember the classes we attended, films we viewed, and horror stories our teachers highlighted about the terrible incidents young people learning to drive were involved in. As authors, we're old enough to remember the days when wearing seat belts was not the norm, when windshields were not made of safety glass, when gas tanks and fuel lines often caught on fire. The losses were terrible: people thrown from cars, disfiguring lacerations, and the incredibly sad stories of children trapped in burning cars. Today, although the same things do happen, with laws and regulations, teaching and technical advancements in cars and trucks, such incidents are fewer.

Imagine the impact of a motor fleet incident from a company perspective. The financial and legal impact of your company driver hitting another car, a pedestrian, a power pole, or a group of children in a school bus may challenge what your company can legally and financially withstand. In some cases, the only defense that you can mount is that you employed trained and properly licensed drivers, you maintained your fleet of vehicles in accordance with best practices and manufacturer's recommendations, and you were following the rules of the road. Failure to validate each of these considerations may severely erode your defense, and the potential for an ever-growing responsibility is real.

Why is fleet safety so important, and why is it discussed here as a special topic? That's easy. Motor vehicle incidents cost employers $60 billion annually in medical and legal considerations, lost time and productivity, and property damage. For those who have any vehicle usage as part of their operations, the *Guidelines for Employers to Reduce Motor Vehicle Crashes* highlights some pretty amazing statistics:

- There is a vehicle crash every 5 seconds.
- There is a vehicle-related injury every 10 seconds.
- Every 12 minutes, someone dies in a motor vehicle crash.[3]

These are amazing numbers, and they should drive you, as an employer, toward an analysis of your vehicle operations and whether they are an integral part your workplace safety program. If motor vehicle operations are excluded from your workplace safety plans, our recommendation is to take the time to integrate safety procedures including training, vehicle inspections, incident investigations, and the like.

The questions you must ask are:

- Is there a return on my vehicle safety investment?
- What are the basic considerations for updating my workplace safety program to include vehicle operations?

Let's take these one at a time.

The guidelines mentioned are from a 2001 Liberty Mutual Insurance Company study. (Liberty Mutual is a well-known property/casualty insurance carrier and one that invests considerable time and money into incident preventioned their companies recouped more than $3.00 for every $1.00 put into their safety efforts, including those within vehicle safety. If you could garner such a return on a financial investment, such as stocks or bonds, we are positive you would not hesitate.

As to how you analyze your vehicle safety efforts and build appropriate elements into your workplace safety program, let's look at several critical considerations.

As noted previously, you must commit to vehicle safety, and your workforce needs to be made part of this process. Without effort and involvement, safety improvements will be compromised. It may be appropriate to include vehicle safety in your workplace safety program's policy statements.

Just as you do with machine guarding, training, and incident investigations, your vehicle safety program must include written policies and procedures. In most respects, these policies and procedures form the foundation for your efforts. We've talked about how important the foundation is to success; don't leave vehicle safety out of that equation.

Administrative activities, such as motor vehicle record checks, reiterating your alcohol and substance abuse polices, and possible screening (required for some types of licenses), should be made part of your program. In addition, incident reporting and investigations are essential parts of your program. Vehicle incidents are no different from incidents involving a foreign object in the eye; both must be reviewed for causation and remediation.

There is no more important issue than vehicle selection, inspections, and maintenance. Scheduled service and inspections are important to include and validate. Ensuring that your drivers can operate assigned vehicles safely is critical as well. Such assurances may mandate specific training and education activities be undertaken. Do not dally on this responsibility; if you have to defend yourself in court, admitting your training program was insufficient or nonexistent will only accrue to a plaintiff's benefit.

Vehicle operations also have important human resources considerations. If a driver fails a drug screen, will they be fired or provided counseling services through an employee assistance program? Depending on the nature of the event, you may have to terminate an employee. Just make sure you have dotted your i's and crossed your t's as to following labor laws and other applicable regulations. For many drivers, counseling and additional training are warranted. Based on the event, we're sure you will know what's best.

Don't forget to consider employee recognition, including rewards (some form of recognition for every 10,000 miles driven without a reportable incident, such as a pin, hat, or jacket) or an incentive program whereby financial benefits may be provided.

Finally, it is your responsibility to ensure that all of your efforts are focused not only on safety but on regulatory compliance as well. For further information on vehicle safety, you can talk to your insurance broker or insurance company. The National Safety Council (www.nsc.org) and NETS (www.trafficsafety.org) are both excellent resources, as are NIOSH and NHTSA (National Highway Traffic Safety Administration).

By looking at construction safety, bloodborne pathogens, trenching and excavations, hazardous energy, and respiratory protection, ergonomics, and vehicle safety, we are only scratching the surface of specific hazards. Dozens of other specific hazards could be reviewed, but we are hopeful that you have focused on the intent of this section. Special control needs and regulations exist because not all hazards are general. Additionally, not all hazards can be controlled through general training; many require very specific training with identified outcome measures. The challenge for many of us is first to recognize the hazards.

One way to recognize hazards, or at least to start establishing the foundation of where hazards may exist, is to perform (as we did in the closed loop analysis) a review of the regulatory mandates that may be found in Fed/OSHA standards or those within your state OSHA requirements, if your state is not managed by Fed/OSHA or has adopted the federal standards. By reviewing the appropriate OSHA standards, either by task or by industry, you will be able to begin structuring a baseline document that focuses on relevant specific or special hazards.

Here are several additional specific hazards that should be recognized by the business professional responsible for safety. This list is not exhaustive, but is intended to provide an overview, beyond those examples just discussed.

Agricultural equipment	Asbestos
Alarm systems	Bulk storage containers

Chainsaws

Confined spaces

Control of hazardous energy
(lock/out-block/out)

Cotton dust

Crane operations

Elevated work surfaces

Emergency evacuation and
procedures

Explosives

Fall protection

Fire extinguishers

Fire safety

First aid and medical
services

Forklifts

Grain-handling facilities

Hazardous materials and
communication

Hazardous waste operations

Lead

Noise

Personal protective equipment

Power presses and machine
guarding

Process safety

Respiratory protection

Storage tanks

Telecommunications

Tree workers

Welding, cutting

Workplace security

Prior to closing our discussion of specific hazards, two additional work-place-related exposures will be included in this chapter's review: *telecom-muting* and *workplace violence*. Specific safety and health regulations for these two concerns can be every difficult to discern. Yet hazards are present from those working at home and from those not capable of dealing with the stressors found at work or in life in general. The latter discussion is critical, in that those employees unable to cope with the stresses of life and work are often those responsible for workplace-violence events.

Telecommuting

In 1999, OSHA published an opinion on telecommuters' safety, indicating that employers must take steps to eliminate work-related safety and health problems (e.g., through on-site visits). This decision was roundly vilified by employers and rescinded a couple of months later.

Both employers and employees can benefit from telecommuting. These benefits may be economic for both employers and for employees, who benefit from being in one of their favorite places: home! But how can the workers' safety be ensured, and do employers have a duty to ensure they are working safely? The only way to manage these concerns is for employees and employers to work together. If OSHA is able to discern that there is an ever-increasing rate of injuries and illnesses from those working at home, it will likely revisit the issue of responsibilities and its own workplace safety standards. At that point, employers may not have a choice but to comply with whatever rules and/or regulations are promulgated.

For an employer, assisting telecommuters with workstation setup and ergonomics is a good first step to reduce safety and health hazards. Providing training will be beneficial as well. Remember, employees who are injured while working at home are still just as unproductive as if they were injured at the company's offices. Employees who work remotely can be assisted with safe working activities in several ways, including through e-mails and the Internet. Staying in touch, even if just by phone, will help retain the (psycho-)social aspect of work and provide a path to communicate discomfort, safety issues, and the need for general assistance.

Although most work-at-home jobs may be safer than many industrial counterparts, you should consider the benefits of how best to assist in maintaining employees' welfare. A question will always arise as to the ultimate responsibility employers have regarding workers' safety while they ply their trade at home. Depending on the nature of the tasks, for example, if the employee drives to the post office to mail documents or go to appointments, an employer responsibility does exist. Further, specific safety and health regulations may have to be followed.

Workplace Violence

Workplace violence has many dimensions, and it arises from both internal and external sources, such as an employee or disgruntled customer. The hazards surrounding such violence must be made part of an ongoing safety and health effort.

Considerable benefits exist from your playing a critical role in safety and health management, especially when considering workplace violence. Many cases of violence have been from unhappy employees, and a myriad of reasons exist for stimulating their violent acts. Layoffs, disciplinary actions, or soured union relationships may be contributing factors. Personal matters such as substance abuse, depression, or other mental disorders may play a contributing role. Regardless of what triggers a violent act, those managing safety and health programs must be prepared for both internal and external threats. In addition, employers must be capable of dealing with threats that come to fruition immediately as well as those that manifest long after a relationship has been ended.

On August 27, 2003, a Chicago man entered his previous place of employment and killed six of its nine employees. The killer had been fired six months prior. It is doubtful that the employees were giving any thought to the killer that day; what is obvious is that the killer had been harassing the business owner and had made previous threats. After killing the workers, the man traded shots with the police and was killed.

Why do we review a case like this? We want to show that not all workplace violence events occur immediately after a termination or disciplinary action. There was a six-month gap between the shooter, Salvador Tapia, being fired and the time he attacked his former coworkers. His firing obviously was not a transition he was capable of managing. The passage of time complicates the safeguards that we must consider. How long after firing a poor performer who had made threats should a company take extraordinary precautions? Of course, the answer will vary with the organization and situation. There are guidelines provided (e.g., by California) on the control of workplace violence, and NIOSH has authored recommended control strategies as well.

Special hazards like workplace violence and telecommuting tell a larger safety and health management story, but one that is consistent with the theme of this book. This is a story of threat recognition and control and the fact that controls are neither always programmed nor simplistic. Significant time had passed in the violence in the workplace scenario, but the business owner had received various communications from Tapia. Should different or special precautions been taken? It's hard to tell. As an employer, you will have to review circumstances such as these on a case-by-case basis. In some situations, it may prove prudent to seek restraining orders and/or hire additional security. But the bottom line is this: In the context of safeguarding your workforce, it may be necessary to adopt special provisions (they are not simple), and these may fall outside of the written regulations found in various OSHA regulations (they are not programmed).

Workplace Security: The Hidden Safety and Health Management Issue

We tend to think of hazards in the workplace in the context of those we have been told about or those where previous injuries have occurred; because of familiarity, our awareness has been heightened. Without the detail associated with rigorous operational reviews, hazards we must control might not be uncovered. Our discussion of the example hazards, further discussions of workplace violence, and the partial list of possible workplace safety programs should suggest to you that your responsibilities toward worker safety and health can be expansive.

Workplace security is an excellent example of a topic worthy of additional discussion. In this context, *workplace security* refers to the larger considerations surrounding violence, possible terrorism, and the many forms that threats in this arena might take.

When considering security, what is hidden most, for example, is the degree to which security should be integrated within a workplace safety program. Those responsible for workplace safety don't purposely subordinate security concerns; it is likely, however, that the issues surrounding security are sufficiently complex to overwhelm such a professional. Think about it: Besides the traditional concerns, such as the theft of assets, there exist threats that may be much more destructive, such as workplace violence, global terrorism, and the economic threats posed by cybersecurity and cyberterror issues. Guidelines, standards, regulations, and laws are being promulgated based on many of these security concerns. You must focus on each area, improving workplace safety programs as necessary.

Recent world events have made the recognition and management of threats job number one for our government and many companies. No longer is terrorism an event that occurs in other parts of the globe; it happens at home and in our backyards. Whether it's terrorism, workplace violence, or managing the company and security workforce, the person managing safety and health must attend to these issues by taking preventive actions and instituting programs, training, and enhanced response capabilities. Simply put, every safety and health or injury and illness prevention program should have a section dedicated to security concerns. As part of focusing your safety efforts, we'll use workplace security as our final example, and expand on it to include additional discussion and a sample program to be used as a guide in the future.

As you review the remainder of this chapter, remember once again our discussion of the Churchill Paradox in Chapter 1. The United States suffered twice at the hands of terrorists. Both events occurred at the World Trade Center (1993 and 2001). In the first, Ramzi Yousef oversaw the placement of a bomb in the parking garage. The second event of September 11, 2001, is etched into our collective memory. Thousands of companies suffer acts of workplace violence every year. Unless our program efforts become stronger and we respond or react much more quickly, the frequency and severity of events will escalate.

Security concerns that should be made part of a workplace safety program, recognizing and controlling threats, include:

- Cyberattacks and cyberterrorism
- Workplace violence
- Terrorism: foreign, domestic, special interest, and so on
- Travel safety, including kidnap and ransom
- Executive protection
- Theft and sabotage
- Facility access: vandalism, malicious mischief, and so on

Protecting an organization from a multitude of security concerns, of course, is the right thing to do, morally and socially. Still, many businesses seek to determine the cost benefits of implementing security measures prior to taking action. Many of us are motivated by the qualitative benefits of security management activities; we can make our case for action based on qualitative measures and incorporate program needs with nothing more. A qualitative measure might be as simple as starting a program, identifying threats, and determining overall organizational vulnerabilities. Each of these measures is sound. Others may be motivated by regulatory mandate. Even in the absence of a specific regulation, the OSHA General Duty Clause may be sufficient to force the employer's hand toward developing specific safety provisions focused on workplace security. This is not to say that many employers have not already undertaken the cause of workplace security and have programs focused on these issues; many have, but many more need to.

For those who need or require quantitative measures, options exist. The

American Society of Industrial Security (ASIS) highlights quantitative measure possibilities in the publication "General Security Risk Assessment Guideline."[4] Methods include forecasting individual loss events, calculating probability or frequency, developing a risk matrix, making probability ratings and lost income cost calculations, and others. The point is, the time needed to become more clear on why security actions are possible and beneficial and the need to prepare a quantitative analysis should not slow a response for an individual responsible for safety and health management. Practical options exist, and can be deployed while a comprehensive assessment is being undertaken.

A unified plan can control many hazards. Such a plan makes managing security-related concerns more practical and makes it possible to overcome hidden program needs.

Growing Concerns: Some Additional Considerations

Globalization and the ease of travel (generally) places many workers and executives in the middle of several security concerns. Executive protection, kidnap and ransom, and travel security in general are issues that must be understood and managed with appropriate rigor. The U.S. Department of State regularly updates a Web site that provides travel warnings and security alerts for global regions, countries, and sometimes even specific airports.[5] Such data should be reviewed before travel to any foreign countries takes place.

It's easy to think of terrorism in foreign lands or against governments. However, terror can be elicited through a person's computer and directed specifically at that person as opposed to an organization. Threats of physical violence, harming one's family, disclosure of secrets, or what is referred to as cyberstalking can all occur through e-mails and Web sites. How to respond and manage threats that have been transmitted in cyberspace should ultimately become part of overall program efforts. Developing a relationship with an organization's information technology department, because of cyberthreats, is essential. Training employees on how to respond to or even interpret threats is becoming more critical as well. What ends up as a physical attack or homicide may have started off as verbal or cyberthreats; controlling them at the outset is the only way to ensure any degree of success in stopping threats from coming to fruition as actual events.

Many of us work for organizations that create strong feelings and responses from any number of people, organizations, and even sometimes terrorist groups. Captive animal programs are a good example. Even those that are designed to perpetuate an endangered species frequently are attacked by their detractors, such as the Animal Liberation Front (ALF). Religious organizations often are attacked by those disagreeing with the basic tenets of the group and who wish to insert their own ideologies.

Special interest terrorism should be a topic of discussion and planning for any organization that conducts operations that raise the ire of a particular group, whether activists or rightists. (It can be argued that all of us are involved in some activities that are the focus of groups that significantly disagree with us.) Minimizing threats from known or potential terrorist action is not a luxury for many organizations; it's becoming a mandate.

Bruce Hoffman in *inside terrorism* highlights this last point several times. His chapter on religion and terrorism is excellent, and ends with this statement: "The pattern of religion-inspired terrorism over the past two years alone suggests that the potential for still more and even greater acts of violence cannot be prudently discounted."[6] Particular focus on the word *prudently*. It will be imprudent for organizations to ignore threats—known or developing. Just as important, organizations need to develop and deploy metrics to recognize threats: again, those that are manifest as well as those that might exist in the future. As we have implied elsewhere in the book, looking forward in order to plan and mitigate developing threats will be the hallmark of a well-run safety and health program.

A critical philosophy hovers over the entire practice of security, whether asset or personal protection. That philosophy is that the cost of protection and controls will be less than that of foreseeable loss. It is possible to plan inappropriately and perhaps over plan. However, most of our efforts will reap tremendous rewards. Critical controls can be implemented that do not fall under the physical control banner. For example, administrative and training controls may be just as important to consider based on the nature of the security threat (e.g., phone or computer threats).

The Selected References and Resources section contains a sample Security Management Plan. It may be beneficial to review that section as you undertake the task of integrating such a plan into your workplace safety program.

As we close this chapter, we ask that you keep in mind the need to look forward in your plan analysis and development efforts. It is essential that you conduct and frequently update threat and hazard analysis to your business's operations, assets, and personnel. By doing so, you can implement corrective and protective actions before a hazard manifests as an injury and/or illness at the individual or group level. Further, recognize that special hazards demand special safety activities, whether they are program components or oriented toward training or hazard mitigation. Successful programs are not static, they are organic. To reiterate our earlier discussions, looking forward and analyzing new operations and processes is the hallmark of the strategic elements of your workplace safety program. In the absence of this capability or effort, your program will become static. From experience, we know that static programs will be utilized less and less frequently, until they wither on the shelf.

If your intention is to truly make a difference in the number and severity of injuries, develop a program that is meaningful and complies with applicable regulations, and, in the process, assists your organization in meeting its goals, then you will become both an excellent strategist and tactician.

BEST PRACTICES

The checklist that follows recaps the critical elements discussed in this chapter and provides you a guide for the analysis and enhancement of your workplace safety efforts. Ask yourself each question. If your answer is "no," "I don't know," or "maybe," you will have to undertake additional research and implement additional safety practices. If the answer is "no," adopt each of the activities as an element of your workplace safety efforts.

Analyzing Your Company's Injuries and Illnesses: Existing and Developing

_____ *Have you reviewed documents (e.g., your First Reports of Injury (Workers' Compensation injury (claims) reports, your OSHA logs and incident investigations) to determine if the injury and illness trends are the result of unsafe acts or unsafe conditions?*

_____ *When adopting a new process or change in operations, do you determine the potential injury and illness outcomes and plan for appropriate safeguards and training?*

_____ Do you have an ongoing process for identifying existing hazards within your company, such as regularly scheduled workplace hazard and activity inspections?

_____ Do internal departments, such as purchasing, operations, and human resources meet to discuss changes in operations and personnel and the potential impact on injury and illness development? Do these departments collectively determine the need for changes or enhancements to your workplace safety program?

Special Hazards

_____ Have you identified the special or unique hazards relative to your business operations? (A sample list of possible hazards is provided in this chapter.)

_____ If an assessment of special hazards has been conducted, have you taken the appropriate steps to either eliminate or control the hazard through engineering, alternate processes, personal protective equipment, or training?

_____ For each special hazard identified, is there a correlating section in your workplace safety program?

_____ For each special hazard, have you identified specific training and education requirements related to the task and its hazards?

_____ Have you identified the specific federal or state OSHA requirements that you must comply with for each of the special hazards?

_____ Have inspection or other hazard assessment tools been modified or developed and employed (i.e., monthly inspections) to ensure that you determine actual employee exposures to special hazards continuously and assess whether they are becoming more severe?

_____ Can you ascertain that each of the elements in the closed loop analysis (Exhibit 4.1) has been addressed?

_____ Do the individuals conducting hazard assessments have the requisite training to conduct a thorough assessment and make meaningful corrective recommendations?

Special Hazard Controls

_____ *Do the hazard controls you have selected for each identified special hazard comply with applicable standards and regulations?*

_____ *Are the controls that you have implemented easily adopted and understood by those who have to implement and/or comply with specific safety measures?*

_____ *If you have workers performing duties at remote sites, have you analyzed their work procedures and identified required hazard controls, training, and possible personal protection equipment needs?*

Special Hazards and Growing Concerns

_____ *Have you adopted a process of regular meetings to review plans for growth into new international markets, fully understanding culturally sensitive considerations?*

_____ *Does your organization conduct international operations or extensive international travel? If so, have you identified the health and security travel hazards?*

_____ *Have you developed an emergency reporting procedure for international or global operations that includes such concerns as medical emergencies, kidnap and ransom, and so forth?*

_____ *Does your company engage in activities that may garner focused attention from activist groups? If so, do you plan for necessary security during critical times, such as announcements, public displays of your goods and services, demonstrations, or speeches and presentations?*

Special Hazard Programs

_____ *Have you developed a security management program that has been made part of your workplace safety efforts?*

CHAPTER 5

Integrating Advanced Topics

As this text has progressed, so has the complexity of the topics. That complexity increases somewhat in this chapter as we integrate three advanced topics we believe all owners and business managers are responsible for workplace safety should be familiar with, understand the relevance to their business operations, and integrate into their workplace safety plans when called for. Two topics are emergency response, crisis, and business continuity planning; and the broad field of risk management. We conclude with some thoughts on moral and ethical considerations in workplace safety management, constituting the third advanced topic.

Many organizations believe that by having emergency response programs, they'll be able to rebuild their organization's productive or service capabilities after a major event, such as a natural or technological disaster. Thinking this way is not only outdated but is also dangerous to your organization's ability to respond and return to operations. Natural disasters, globally as well as within the United States, have clearly borne this fact out. Hurricanes Katrina and Rita both slammed into the Gulf Coast in the fall of 2005. Mississippi and Louisiana were especially hard hit. Months after the hurricanes ravaged Pascagoula, Biloxi, New Orleans, and dozens of other cities and towns, hundreds of thousands were still without homes and thousands of businesses hadn't reopened their doors. Many will never return to what they called home, and many, if not most, of the businesses will ever reopen.

The inability to reoccupy or reopen a business after a truly catastrophic event may be beyond the control of the homeowner or the business, but in most cases, both have something to say about how quickly they get back up and running. This capability, just like worker safety, is structured around analysis, program development, and training. We highlight each of these considerations in this chapter.

Many business professionals, even those with significant training, confuse workplace safety and risk management. We feel it is vital to spend a few paragraphs on distinguishing the two. They are related and benefit from each other, but they are not one and the same. In this chapter, we distinguish the critical characteristics of risk management and encourage you to enhance any planning efforts you have made or to integrate risk management activities into your workplace safety plans.

Moral and ethical considerations underpin workplace safety. We'd like to think that everyone shares our moral obligations toward safeguarding our fellow workers' safety and health, but unfortunately we have been and suspect we will be disappointed again. To a large extent, we feel the discussion surrounding moral and ethical considerations constitutes an advanced topic; as you read through the case studies, you'll understand why.

The three topics in this chapter are advanced because they are avoided or given short shrift in the analysis, planning and deployment, and training aspects of emergency plans. Likely this lack of attention is based, at least for emergency response and business recovery planning and risk management, on the fact that neither is a particularly easy subject. However, today's work environment requires you give both of these topics consideration and adopt critical, relevant components within your workplace safety plan or related programs.

The authors have conducted literally thousands of workplace reviews, safety surveys, training classes, and incident investigations. We continue to be stymied as to why some employers choose to neglect even the most basic safety requirements. Some avoid activities because they feel they are too costly; others feel that "something bad won't happen to them"; and, of course, in rare cases, employers simply do not care about the welfare of their workers. Like us, the government also believes that the topic is serious enough to establish laws surrounding the unethical treatment of workers and the abandonment of safety protocols.

As you read this chapter, it is incumbent upon you to recall what you have learned earlier: analyze, mitigate, plan, train, and update. Whether it's basic safety considerations, emergency management, or risk management, the mantra holds true. Take one step at a time, and you will be successful.

EMERGENCIES AND RELATED PLANNING AND RESPONSE

Consider the national and global events that garnered massive media attention in the last several years. Seldom, if ever, is the impact of such events restricted to the locale where they occurred. Whether events were natural, technological, human-precipitated, or contingent (social) in origin, their effects are most always far reaching. A company that goes out of business in San Diego, California, due to an earthquake, may displace workers in other states who work for companies supplying raw materials and component parts.

What types of events fall into such categories? Earthquakes, wildfires, hurricanes, and other weather-related occurrences are examples of natural events that may portend emergencies, crises, and even disasters. Workplace violence, sabotage, and even terrorism fall under the umbrella of man-made or human-precipitated events. Malicious computer code and viruses, though human in origin, along with systems-driven processes, are some possible technological concerns. Social reaction to political events, such as picketing and rioting, is a contingent threat that business owners and companies must be prepared for.

Although these threats and their outcomes are disparate, we have found that people, businesses, and the governments that have to respond attempt unify them for response purposes. Events, such as those noted in the paragraph above are disparate. It is critical that the capabilities of individuals, businesses, and the government to recognize the threats they will face and develop meaningful plans to respond and recover from them should they manifest, be actively developed and tested.

The role of those vested with workplace safety management responsibilities, then, is becoming more and more critical. They must:

- Identify specific vulnerabilities within the natural, technological, human-precipitated, and contingent categories.
- Recommend threat mitigation and control options.

- Lead the charge with related employee training and education.

- Ensure that threat response and recovery procedures are in place and up-to-date.

Real or Potential Magnitude Equates to Involvement

If we look at the magnitude of the New York World Trade Center attacks on September 11, 2001, they were staggering by any measure. So too were the 2005 hurricanes. What was astonishing, though, in New York was the number of organizations that were fully operational some six weeks after an event unparalleled in our nation's history. Some of these organizations had rigorously tested emergency response, crisis management, and disaster recovery plans, but not all. Many companies survived because their management teams remained intact; thus managers were in place to make some tough decisions and ensure ongoing operations.

Historically, very few organizations invest the time to critically evaluate technical, human, natural, or contingent threats that they might face. This lack of focus on threat identification and analysis is reflected in poor response and recovery planning. Within the applied aspects of emergency, crises, and disaster management, organizations distinguish themselves. The combined efforts of analyzing threats (see the Threat Matrix in Selected References and Resources), qualifying and quantifying their impact (should they manifest), and developing necessary emergency response, crisis management, and business resumption plans are generally referred to as business continuity plans. Research has shown that organizations that actively analyze threats (recognition) and develop meaningful response and recovery plans generally fare better than those that don't plan. Studies at Oxford University are often cited as some of the better historic models.[1]

The Oxford studies looked at the time to regain shareholder value from recoverers as opposed to nonrecoverers (those who had planned versus those who had not). Recovery time for shareholder value was within 50 days for those who prepared for event response; for those who did not, recovery time was consistently more than a year. In fact, the initial shareholder loss following an event for recoverers was about 5 percent, while it was more than twice that for nonrecoverers.

Business Continuity Management

As noted, the ability to recognize, respond, and recover from threats that have manifested is largely found in the practice of business continuity management (often called simply business continuity or continuity planning). We'll continue to use the umbrella term *business continuity management* to integrate the distinct elements of emergency preparedness, crisis management, and business recovery.

Before expanding on the basics of business continuity management, ask yourself these questions:

- Is your organization in an area subject to any particular natural threat?
- Are you reliant on technologies that, if interrupted, pose a significant business interruption?
- Are you subject to sabotage and/or malicious attacks based on your operations?
- Have you led your organization through an analysis of possible scenarios you may face, now and in the future?

Okay, let's assume you answered "yes" to one or more of the initial questions and "no" to the last. If that's the case, keep reading!

There is an old adage that goes something like this: "You cannot respond to that which you do not identify." At the very least, it's difficult to respond effectively. Threat identification includes both qualitative (categories) and quantitative measures (how frequent and how large). This effort is essential so that you can prioritize response and recovery protocols that correlate. Professional business continuity planners frequently refer to this aspect of business continuity management as the *risk and business impact assessment*. Thus, in the assessment or recognition phase of business continuity, the intent is to identify and categorize threats and determine the likely impact on your organization should one or more of the threats actually take place.

Threats must be delineated within meaningful categories for two important reasons. First, by categorizing threats, you can distinguish between them; second, through categorization, you are able to clarify response procedures and recovery needs, making them as specific as might be required.

Most organizations develop categories of threats instinctively or borrow from known sources, such as risk management departments or insurance carriers. As a starting point, threats might be categorized as natural threats, technological, human or man-made, and contingent.

Natural threats emanate, of course, from the natural environment. Earthquakes, floods, hurricanes, wildfires, tsunamis, and other weather-related issues are all examples of natural threats. Information technology (IT), IT infrastructures, software, telecommunications, and one-of-a-kind production equipment are some areas that technological threats might affect.

Depending on the nature of your operations, human or man-made threats may predominate. You must evaluate security concerns while traveling—kidnap and ransom, extortion and fraud, violence, sabotage, and terrorism, among others—to determine what your organization can do to mitigate, control, and respond to such events. Human threats abound; consider captive American workers in Iraq and bus explosions in Britain. Bad things do happen to good companies and good people; our job, within the confines of our workplace safety program, is to be ready for them and to respond accordingly.

What are contingent threats? Contingent threats are those whose occurrence is a function of external events over which you have little or no control. Further, contingent threats often originate in the social realm. Picketing, for example, that has nothing to do with your operations but disrupts incoming shipments may be thought of as a contingent threat. If your business is next door to a lab conducting experiments on animals, you are likely at risk of the (contingent) threat of an activist or rightist group focused on disrupting those operations.

Think of what happened as the outcome of the Rodney King trials became known. Most of us remember the riots, the looting, the fires, and the images of Reginald Denny being pulled from his truck and beaten severely. Mr. Denny had nothing to do with the Rodney King decision; he was just in the wrong place at the wrong time. How does this story relate to our organizational or business perspective? Could shop owners who were miles from the epicenter of the initial outbreak of violence have anticipated that such an event would take place and that their shops would be looted and burned? The outcomes were clearly contingent on an event that arose from the social realm. The potentials were difficult to assess as part of a threat assessment endeavor, and pre-event mitigating actions were nearly impossible to determine.

In the end, by including contingent threats as a threat category, we are encouraging organizations to play a very robust game of "what if." By doing so, organizations likely will make more detailed assessments of natural, technological, and human threats. Planning for the unknown and "unthinkable" will become part of their business continuity processes.

Threat recognition and identification must be ongoing. There are significant reasons for making threat recognition one of the most vital aspects of overall business continuity planning efforts. Threats mutate. They change. Those that were once inconsequential can become critical overnight. The frequency of threat identification activities changes as threat triggers change. For example, changes in operations, locations, key personnel, suppliers, weather events, and activities at competitors are all triggers. All of these events or possible events should trigger review efforts. At the least, you should analyze threats annually, but if something has changed, why wait?

If you have done a good job of identifying threats to your operations and assessed their potential magnitude, your next step is to develop emergency response protocols. Emergency response efforts are those that take place in the first minutes and hours after an event. Some are general and apply to many threats, while others are designed to respond to specific events.

The bridge between emergency response and recovery from an event rests with crisis management and communication. Crisis management involves efforts that include event management, leadership, and decision making. Additionally, an enhanced and specific communication capability must be established. These efforts are rigorous and usually require a focused location to be established. Such locations, which can be mobile or fixed, are generally referred to as emergency operations or crisis management centers.

The last tactical step of business continuity is business recovery. Steps necessary to ensure continuity of operations, such as prenegotiated partnerships and access to recovery equipment, assets, and personnel, are often undertaken to effect a meaningful plan.

Emergency Response

An organization's emergency response plan defines how the organization actually will manage its response to an emergency. This review focuses on that initial tactical element and the role that you may have to assume to ensure success. Organizations cannot jump from event recognition to full business recovery. The steps of emergency response and crisis management must usually be traversed before there can be any hope of meaningful business recovery.[2]

An emergency response plan must address two critical issues. The first issue relates to the comprehensiveness of the threat assessment previously conducted. The better the threat assessment, the more specific your emergency response plans can be, ultimately resulting in a quicker, more efficient and meaningful response. Some events lend themselves to general response guidelines (e.g., building evacuations or calling for emergency personnel); other mandate specific emergency response protocols (e.g., many threats to information systems and technology threats as well as numerous human and natural threats). For example, general response guidelines may not be sufficient to safeguard employees in the event of an armed robbery or a chemical spill. Workplace safety professionals often are involved in and/or oversee emergency response activities. These tactical activities frame the second critical issue of an emergency response plan.

Remember, emergency response plans are designed to guide an organization through the first minutes and possibly hours after to an event. Rarely do emergency response activities go beyond a few hours. When faced with an emergency, standard operating procedures are no longer valid, and emergency procedures must be invoked. Thus, much of emergency response was born out of the need to make rapid plan implementation decisions in order minimize injuries, loss of life, and physical damage as well as organizational liabilities. Many lessons have been learned from past events. One of the difficult lessons has been to overcome the thought (and thus, the lack of preparation) that emergency response is relegated to professionally trained personnel, such as fire, emergency medical, and police agencies. These professionals occupy a critical role, but the real success of your planning efforts becomes evident before the professionals arrive.

As you review your emergency response planning efforts, consider:

- Do plans correlate to the threats you've identified?
- Will personnel need specialized response training?
- Does your plan include necessary communication equipment and methodologies?

- Are those people assigned specific responsibilities and accountabilities available? If not, have backups been assigned and trained?

For plans to succeed, emergency communications must be a focal point of planning. Initial communications are what often activate an emergency response plan. It is important to recognize in the initial stages of an event that communication may not necessarily be verbal. A horn, a klaxon, or a bullhorn, even a written message via e-mail may be the triggering communication to begin emergency response efforts. For example, an e-mail may be the trigger event to begin procedures for managing a foodborne illness, terrorism, or a comment in an industry or trade journal.

As you begin your emergency plan analysis and developmental activities, keep these practical considerations in mind:

- Your plan should include a system to notify key personnel, whether they are within the facility or off-site. With cellular technologies, satellite communication, and advanced paging systems, there should be no problem in notifying all essential emergency response personnel immediately and en masse.

- Those who have specific duties, such as facilities management and emergency response coordinators, must not only be available but must have access to programs and protocols, no matter where the individuals are located. Again, with the use of basic technologies, these personnel should be able to assist with response efforts from home or remote locations. Access to networked or server-based programs and programs stored on laptops or personal digital assistants (PDAs) will enable individuals to respond to emergencies.

- Your emergency response plans must have some basic goals. First among them may be moving personnel to safe areas, accounting for everyone and their well-being, and determining in advance what your organization will do if someone is unaccounted for. This is important, for example, to keep fellow employees from rushing back into a burning or collapsing structure to look for someone who may have taken the day off.

- Your emergency response plan must include instructions on the efforts to be taken if a fellow employee is trapped in a building. Why is this important? If a decision has been made that in every case you will send personnel into a structure to look for lost or trapped employees, then those assuming that search and rescue role will need to participate in specialized training. Although there may be sound reasons for having your own search and rescue team, in most cases it may be best to leave such activities to the professionals.

Regardless of the category of threat—natural, technical, human, or contingent—general and specific response protocols should be developed. To ensure the protocols are both practical and safe, build exercises in the forms of case studies, tabletop analyses, and functional drills into your overall planning efforts. Help with exercises and drills often can be obtained from your insurance agent or broker, carrier, or public service agencies.

Which Exercise Format Do You Use?

Case studies create awareness and can help set the tone for organizational emergency response goals. Since case studies tend to be narrative discussions that are read, they provide no practical application per se. Although case studies are a great way to begin analyzing capabilities, their lack of an applied aspect limits their benefit to the awareness level. Clearly, the limitations of case studies cannot be tolerated when preparing and practicing critical response protocols.

Tabletop analyses will help take your organization to the next level of capability. In many cases, however, the lack of functional interruption— that is, truly simulating an impact on your business operations—will again leave you a tad short of truly testing your response capabilities. The value of tabletops rests largely with the teamwork that is required to complete such exercises. And, in fact, tabletop exercises can be fairly aggressive, evaluating teamwork, communication networks, access to plans, some technologies, as well as other plan elements.

Functional exercises, which may be either large or small scale, are the pinnacle of testing your plan's capabilities to help see you through an emergency or worse. These exercises are intended to simulate to the fullest extent possible actual emergencies and to test response capabilities. The utilization of outside evaluators in such events is often recommended. Their unbiased views may enable you to develop plan improvements that make a difference in a real-world emergency.

Depending on the nature of the threat and your assessment of the likelihood of its occurrence, your plan tests may need to be more than the typical annual review. Weekly for most (but not all!) is too frequent. Once a month for other threats is just right, and annually for some is okay too. The frequency and rigor of plan tests and exercises dependent on the frequency and potential magnitude of particular threats and your recovery time objectives.

Crisis Management

Crisis management (and communications) serves as the strategic and tactical bridge between emergency response and business recovery efforts.[3] As with negotiating any valley or river, a sound bridge makes that journey much easier. To the outside observer, crisis management and communication efforts are typically transparent, in spite of the fact that the scene of an event and headquarters are likely to be beehives of activity.

Crisis management encompasses event management, including decision making and leadership. Some flexibility exists in the models employed to ensure sound crisis management, but consistent elements within these models include:

- Planning
- Operations
- Logistics
- Financial considerations

Together, these categories are the mainstays of what's referred to as the incident command system, which is a discussion beyond the scope of this book.[4]

Once emergency response efforts have been under way and the dynamics of an event are understood, larger-scale planning to coordinate the efforts of various responding parties is begun. For planning efforts to be effective, information must be gleaned from several sources. These sources include, for example, operations and human resources. Often such information is analyzed and synthesized in a central location.

Many organizations and most governmental bodies use a command center of some sort to coordinate crisis management (and communications) activities. The command centers or, as they are frequently referred to, emergency operations centers (EOCs) serve as the hub of activities. In some cases, field EOCs are utilized in place of and/or in addition to an EOC at a fixed location. Such is the case with the airlines. They often establish site-located EOCs subsequent to a crash and maintain a fixed EOC at their headquarters.

EOCs provide a base for systematic strategy development and the best place to ensure that all elements of event management are being considered and carried out. In large-scale or long-term events, such as a natural disaster, the September 11 events in New York, or the wildfires in San Diego County in 2004 (the state's largest fire ever), logistical (acquisition of supplies and equipment that support operations) and financial needs are determined, event management is planned, and operational needs are assessed at the EOC.

EOCs are real; they contain communications equipment and supplies, such as food, water, hygiene, and comfort, as well as administrative tools that may last for days. These may include maps, satellite images, computers, radios, and televisions; all can be found in more advanced EOCs. Many organizations do not use an EOC-like structure in order to save money. Others don't employ EOCs due to a lack of understanding of their use and value. However, the functions of an EOC can be structured on a shoestring, and EOCs can be operated from remote locations. What's most important, though, is that the functions found within an EOC are made part of your organization's plans.

Look at a natural disaster, for example; in most events, it is unlikely that the EOC would be operational prior to the disaster occurring (though it certainly could be). When should an EOC be activated? There are four times you should consider:

Preemptive activation. If, for example, a hurricane is moving toward your operations and landfall is likely, there may be flooding and infrastructure interruption. Don't wait for the flooding and power outages to occur to activate the EOC. By activating it ahead of time, you can more quickly ensure that plans are in place, resources are mustered, and personnel are prepared to do their jobs.

Threat-dependent activation. In many cases when an organization has received a threat, especially one that cannot quickly be discounted, activation of the EOC may be in order. In times of heightened alert, it is possible for EOCs to be activated in anticipation of a threat manifesting for days on end.

Event-dependent activation. In a natural, technological, human, or contingent event—an emergency, crisis, or disaster—your EOC needs to be activated. In some cases, events can be managed from an executive's or manager's office. It is however, prudent, to activate the EOC.

Practice or training activation. Activating an EOC and all of the activities that are conducted within the EOC must be practiced with some regularity. Certainly do so upon initial development. Other training activation times may include changes in essential personnel, technology modifications, identification of new threats, regulatory demand, and after an event (especially if some event management aspects did not go well and there is a need to improve them).

Communicating in a Crisis

Crisis communications includes communicating with both internal and external constituents. Many organizations spend a great deal of time communicating externally with the media, regulators, and stakeholders. Often these communication activities take place to the exclusion of their own human resources. In other cases, companies communicate with employees but bury their heads in the sand hoping to avoid communicating with the many external constituents who may have legitimate (and in many cases, legal) needs to hear and know how an event is being managed.

Crisis communications in the context of business continuity management include:

- Internal and external communication requirements
- Message content and context
- Form of communication utilized
- Tools of communication

The EOC is a great place to ensure that communications strategies are being employed by the right individuals at the right times and with appropriate messages. The EOC, however, is not the best place to conduct communication activities primarily with external constituents. Think of it this way: "Would you like a representative of the media in your EOC?" We do not pose this question to imply that you should deny media access to your organization in an emergency, crisis, or disaster. We do recommend, however, that media interactions or other communication activities not related to the EOC take place outside the EOC.

Not communicating with the media may result in harsh focus being placed on an organization (as witnessed in the Sago mine disaster of January 2, 2006). The media can actually help carry messages, and positive relationships can and should be nurtured. It is essential that you consider who will speak to the media as much as where communications will take place. Of course, it's advantageous to have trained personnel interact with special publics, such as the media.

Many companies have advanced communication capabilities. Radios, satellite phones, secure e-mail and Web sites, and paging systems that can keep large numbers of personnel up-to-date on an event at all times are available. All of these devices, and many more, comprise an everwidening technological pool for communicating in an emergency, crisis, or disaster. Their use and availability must be planned for. Yet just as these methods of communication can help an organization, they can work against it as well.

For example, confidential subjects must be discussed over secure lines. Cell phones and many two-way radio transmissions are not secure. Organizations can overcome some of this problem by communicating in prescribed codes, such as "10-codes." Since many listeners may know 10-codes, it may be in an organization's best interest to ensure secure communication links for internal and external discussions.

Business or Operational Recovery

Business recovery may be considered the systematic recovery of the most critical (or otherwise identified) operations of an organization, facility, or department. To that end, and in formal business continuity endeavors, business recovery is one of the strategic (and, upon implementation, tactical) components of such planning.

These factors include (among many others):

- *Criticality of operations.* Some operations or aspects of operations may not fail under any circumstances. This may be the case of the power infrastructure to hospitals and other critical care facilities. Thus, recovery and business continuation needs are relatively immediate.

When these critical operations are being considered, all redundant capabilities must be analyzed as well.

- *Contractual obligations or requirements.* Business continuity plans must be evaluated from the perspective of obligations or contractual mandates. There may be many ways to provide contracted or otherwise obligated services, such as through subcontracting. If this is the case, though, the ability of the subcontractor must become part of the overall review.

- *Life safety.* If operations must be maintained to ensure life safety or the welfare of personnel, or if an organization is responsible for the provision of services related to life safety, continuity plans must be capable of meeting minimally defined needs. These needs may be the availability of backup safety or medical supplies at one end of the scale, or access to a C–130 cargo plane to ship supplies to a regional disaster at the other end of the scale.

- *Revenue streams.* For many organizations, revenue streams have become so tight that the smallest of disruptions may jeopardize their survival. Recovery capabilities of software and data processing equipment to process accounts receivables, then, should become part of the recovery evaluation for such organizations.

- *Supply chain dependency.* Warehouses are, for many organizations, a thing of the past. Supplies enter the processing chain just as they are needed and spend as little time as possible at a facility prior to being shipped or picked up as a finished good or component part. If an organization relies on certain suppliers, then its plan would be vastly improved if agreements could be structured to include secondary suppliers. Supply chain dependency becomes more critical if a supplier or other provider is a sole source; who will provide the service or goods if a sole source supplier is unable to do so?

Validating Emergency Response, Crisis Management, and Business Recovery Capabilities

It is impossible to know whether an organization's emergency response, crisis management, and business recovery plans can function unless they are tested with some regularity. Tests, drills, and/or exercises are all valuable and should be made part of your overall program.

Tests of plans are also referred to as drills or exercises, although there may be some delineation based on the rigor of the test. Again, for the purposes of this discussion, we use the terms *test, drill,* and *exercise* to mean the same thing. Once a plan has been created, the prudent thing to do is evaluate whether the elements of the plan work.

Individual components of a plan, for example, may be evaluated, or the ability of personnel to perform certain functions within a plan may be determined. Tests may encompass single locations and specific threats (e.g., many tests were conducted in preparation for Y2K concerns) or be general and enterprise-wide. However, for tests to be beneficial, they must be capable of:

- Evaluating all aspects of an organization's business continuity and crisis management plan
- Evaluating the ability and capabilities of essential emergency response or crisis management staff
- Determining that access to recovery supplies and equipment is unencumbered
- Confirming that plan-specific crisis communication strategies and tactics are deployable
- Confirming that recovery partners can meet their requirements whenever called on

Tests, drills, or exercises may take one of the forms noted earlier in the chapter. The more critical the operations are to manage and the more quickly they need to be recovered, the more robust the plans should be. If an organization is simply attempting to check the validity of a response protocol, a case study may be employed. If a need exists to ensure the functionality of an emergency operations center, small- and/or large-scale exercises may be in order. Regardless of the nature of the test, aspects identified as needing enhancement must find their way into an organization's business continuity and crisis management plan.

Maintaining Your Plans

What are the plan maintenance and update triggers? There are several, and they generally follow safety and health program strategies. Certainly, plans should be reviewed and updates or improvements made subsequent to any emergency, crisis, or disaster response. Some other plan maintenance triggers to consider include:

- Changes in operations or an increase in the distributed nature of operations
- A recognition in the changing nature of particular threats, either from research, information exchange, similar companies' experiences, or warnings from government agencies
- Any time new personnel arrive who will play an essential role in a business continuity and crisis management program
- Subsequent to plan tests, drills, or exercises where improvement needs have been identified
- At the very least, annually

The ability to meet the most basic demands in the future may well rest on whether an organization can respond to emergencies, tackle the variety of crises that it will face, and overcome disasters, all while maintaining a predetermined semblance of operations. It is essential then that organizations do what is right from a planning perspective now—not later. Unplanned emergency response is rarely successful. Experiences and data accumulated by many suggest there is no better time than now to enhance your business continuity and crisis management capabilities. Get plans right through planning and practice, not by simply surviving an event. Business continuity and crisis management can and will help organizations meet many of their goals and objectives, now and in the future.

RISK MANAGEMENT

Risk management is not the same as workplace safety management, and vice versa. Risk is related to the measure of frequency and severity of events. A hazard (the fundamental nature of something to cause harm) that is not manifested has no risk associated with it. There is some latitude in that thought, however. Risk management does consider the ultimate impact of certain events, and the practice guides managers into determining if conducting operations with certain risks (outcomes) is in their best interests. If a specific task is not undertaken, then there are no hazards and no operational safety measures that need to be undertaken.

Risk management formally is "the process of making and implementing decisions that will minimize the adverse effects of accidental and business losses on an organization."[5]

The practice of risk management is a formal one, and various professional designations can be earned, such as the Associate in Risk Management (ARM), which is conferred by the Insurance Institute of America subsequent to passing a series of national examinations. Risk management is broken in two primary directions: risk control and risk financing. Safety management, of course, falls mostly in the former, while workers' compensation and other insurance programs, such as financing tools, are included in the latter.

Basic Definitions

As we continue our discussion of risk management, keep these definitions in mind:

- *Exposure avoidance.* Eliminates a specific loss exposure and is the self-sufficient risk management technique. Exposure avoidance has very limited applications, but should be the first option in analyzing possible choices in your organization's management program.

- *Loss prevention.* Any method that reduces the probability or frequency of a specific loss. Loss prevention does not completely eliminate the possibility of loss exposure.

- *Loss reduction.* Techniques that reduce the severity of those losses that do occur. Preloss measures (applied before the loss occurs) and post-loss measures (applied after the loss occurs) are the broad categories encompassing loss reduction.

- *Segregation.* Aims to reduce an organization's dependence on a single asset, activity, or person. The two forms of segregation are (1) separation and (2) duplication.

- *Contractual transfer.* Involves the transfer of loss exposure from one party to another. Contractual transfer for risk control and contractual transfer for risk financing are two common methods of contractual transfer.[6]

These definitions serve as the core elements and strategies of risk management. More information on each is provided as the chapter unfolds.

Risk management in many respects revolves around the design of approaches to create acceptable risk within an organization operationally, financially, and legally. In addition, effective risk management programs help organizations avoid activities that create unacceptable risk. Professional risk managers measure risk in several ways, including what they and their organizations believe to be morally acceptable. Other strategies include analyzing the impact of certain activities on operations (should something go wrong), straight financial analysis, and sometimes complicated enterprise-wide risk analyses including the use of various modeling techniques, such as Monte Carlo simulations. On the whole, risk management attempts to go well beneath the surface in analyzing the impact of operations, events, and certain losses on an organization.

Categories of Risk

Risk falls within four categories:

Property

Liability

Personnel

Financial[7]

The assumption is that anything that carries "risk" will fit within one of these categories. For the most part we agree. We have seen, however, successful programs where the categories were made much more discrete (specific). Other categories of risk utilized include individual, natural, technological, human, and strategic, for example.

Risk management goes on to determine what assets, or things of value in an organization, may be exposed to loss and then defines the peril causing that loss. Risk management then determines as fully as possible the potential financial impacts. Risk, then, by definition is the measure of the probability of an event or its outcome and the resulting severity.

Risk Management Cascade

Risk management does not stop at determining what an organization might be exposed to. The practice seeks to determine if alternatives exist that carry less risk. An option felt to be best is tested and monitored and, if need be, modified or abandoned. The process can be viewed as a cascade of actions and decisions, as shown in Exhibit 5.1.

There is a feedback loop or cycle aspect to making risk management decisions. Decisions (selecting the best option) are based on analysis, not relegated simply to intuition or, much worse, guessing. Once a decision has been made to deploy a certain approach to managing a risk, it has to be evaluated and, if need be, altered.

Approaches to Risk Management: Options

In risk management, once options for controlling a risk have been reviewed, one has to be selected and implemented. What are the options and how do they function?

Our discussion will focus on the risk control options most risk managers consider, as they are linked more strongly to the day-to-day safety and health activities that we've been discussing. The options were outlined in the definitions at the beginning of the chapter. Let's look at the potential benefits and drawbacks of each.

- *Exposure avoidance.* Some exposures or activities we might want to engage in have the potential to create so much "risk" that the best choice might be to avoid the exposure altogether. Although this is a default approach for many, choosing it obviously does not allow an organization to benefit from an activity that might reap rewards. Approach activities by asking yourself this question: "Should the (particular) activity be avoided?"

- *Loss prevention.* Another option, and one that is utilized often, is loss prevention. In fact, loss prevention and loss reduction are the hallmarks of the safety function. Loss prevention is dedicated to reducing the frequency of an adverse outcome; it does not attempt to reduce all of the exposures to a particular loss. For example, the use

---

EXHIBIT 5.1   RISK MANAGEMENT CASCADE

1. Identify exposures.
  2. Examine control options.
    3. Select the best option.
      4. Implement the option.
        5. Monitor, follow up, and make changes.

of hearing protection in a noisy environment, if the appropriate type and worn properly, will protect a worker from injury. The use of hearing protection, however, does nothing to modify the amount of ambient noise in the environment.

- *Loss reduction.* Loss reduction techniques, however, attempt to minimize the severity of any loss. By lowering the amount of noise at the source, the potential severity of hearing loss can be reduced as well.

- *Segregation.* Certain operations, machines, and skills are so essential that an organization is significantly impacted if they are disrupted, damaged, or harmed. When such criticality exists, a risk manager has to look at other options to implement. One of the options within segregation is the separation of assets exposed to loss. For example, if machine A is extremely valuable to an operation's success, it can be separated and thereby protected from other hazardous operations. Separation, in space and time, is used frequently for personnel to restrict them from extremely hazardous operations. (Blasting, nuclear energy, and oxygen-deficient atmospheres are examples.)

- *Duplication.* Duplication provides the risk manager with another level of redundancy. Some operations are so essential that they must be mirrored. (Such mirroring is a common tactic deployed in the information technology field.) In these cases, the Risk Manager plays a critical role in ensuring the safety and protection of each party or asset (from a personnel and a physical protection standpoint).

- *Contractual transfer for risk control.* Simply, this implies that a particular hazardous operation, or one that might have unacceptable risk, is contractually transferred to another party. Contractual transfer is frequently an option where extreme hazards exist, such as working on elevated platforms and in confined spaces. Many employers recognize the risks but need the particular operations to continue to achieve revenues or meet contractual obligations. As they do not wish for their employees to be at risk, they outsource the task to a specialist.

- *Contractual transfer for financing.* This is a technique where the economic burden for loss is transferred to another party. Such is the case in a workers' compensation insurance policy. This policy is a contract, shifting much of the economic burden of employee injuries to the insurance company.

Risk control techniques within risk management are similar to those found in workplace safety. Combining the efforts of the two will strengthen the overall safety and health management plan of an organization. Risk management also encompasses the field of risk financing. Generally, the financial aspect of events, such as costs associated with injuries, illnesses, fines, vehicle incidents, and so forth, can be treated in the same way as risk control. In risk financing, financial exposures can either be retained or they can be transferred.

MORAL AND ETHICAL CONSIDERATIONS IN WORKPLACE SAFETY

Employees expect, and demand, that they are safe while working. Working is an essential part of modern existence; an important activity in which people participate. The confluence of work and workers and the moral and ethical issues facing employers can be divided into various categories.

Social Responsibility and Work Health

Business social responsibility consists of private and voluntary (personal and company) initiatives that complement government action and financial efforts. Business social responsibility means many things to many people. To us, most of all, it strikes at the heart of what is the voluntary process: a complement to the legislative process. Companies that acknowledge this fact recognize that there is more to be gained both ethically and commercially from caring appropriately about their workforce.

Will people choose jobs with organizations and buy products from companies because of policies on workplace safety and other ethical reasons, such as fair trade practices? (The Fair Trade Federation [FTF] is an association of fair trade wholesalers, retailers, and producers whose members are committed to providing fair wages and good employment opportunities to economically disadvantaged artisans and farmers worldwide. FTF directly links low-income producers with consumer markets and educates consumers about the importance of purchasing fairly traded products that support living wages and safe and healthy conditions for workers in the developing world.)

For some industries, a company's safety reputation can impact heavily on the demands for its products and the level of its share price. For example, one survey found that 69 percent of respondents said they would consider investing their money in a socially responsible fund. In Australia, the Australian Financial Services Reform Act of 2001 requires the seller or issuer of investment products to disclose to investors the extent (if at all) to which labor standards (safety and health) and other social or ethical considerations are taken into account in the investment selection.

By stating your company's social responsibility and voluntary commitments to safety (ones that go beyond regulatory and conventional requirements), you raise the standards of social development, environmental protection, and respect of fundamental health and safety rights of all working people.

Implementing company social responsibility needs commitment from top management. Also needed is innovative thinking, new skills, and closer involvement of the employees and their representatives in a two-way dialogue that can structure permanent feedback and adjustment.

Legal and Regulatory Considerations

Workplace safety has improved steadily since the early 1970s, when the federal government started to promote safety and to demand that states and local governments take actions.

Companies have a legal obligation to inform employees of the Occupational Safety and Health Act (OSHA) safety and health standards that apply to their workplace. Upon request, an employer must make available copies of those standards and the OSHA law itself.

Under OSHA, employers have a general duty (the general duty clause) to provide work and a workplace free from recognized hazards. Citations may be issued by OSHA when violations of standards are found and for violations of the general duty clause (even if no specific OSHA standard applies to the particular hazard). In addition, each employer must display (in a prominent place) the official OSHA poster that describes rights and responsibilities under the act.

Possible Criminal Penalties

Public protection laws allow for managers to be criminally prosecuted as individuals for the actions of their businesses. And they can serve jail time for company violations, even though they had no direct role in the crime.

Most of these convictions are based on statutes and regulatory provisions known as public welfare legislation. Some of these cases demonstrate how managers can be prosecuted for failure "to use reasonable care." No comprehensive list of statutes that impose strict liability on businesspeople exists; however, in general, their common goal is to protect the public, and prevent incidents and injuries by exercising a reasonable level of care.

It would be wise to familiarize yourself with the laws of jurisdiction in which you conduct business. Often states enact similar statutes. Two landmark cases provide examples of state law that further defines ethical and criminal conduct:

- *1983: Film Recovery Systems (FRS).* FRS was in the business of recovering silver from film negatives. This was done by placing the negatives into vats of cyanide. Hydrogen cyanide gas would bubble up from the vats. Ten minutes after collapsing near a vat of cyanide, Stefan Golab, 61, died of cyanide poisoning. He did not speak English, nor was he advised of the dangers of his work.

  In this case, company officials (including the company president, the plant manager, and the plant foreman) were convicted of manslaughter and sentenced to prison. The prosecution was able to show that the three executives knew of the dangers that the worker was exposed to and that they further understood that their failure to provide protective equipment created a strong probability of death or great bodily harm.

  In a review of the case, the grand jury charged five defendants with murder, stating that, as individuals and as officers and high managerial agents of FRS, they had, on February 10, 1983, knowingly created a strong probability of Golab's death. Generally, the indictment stated that the individual defendants failed to disclose to Golab that he was working with substances containing cyanide and failed to advise him, train him to anticipate, and provide adequate equipment to protect him from attendant dangers involved. The grand jury charged FRS and the managers with involuntary manslaughter.

- *1999: L.E. Myers Co. and its parent, MYR Group Inc.* On May 20, 2005, in a rare criminal case, L.E. Myers was found guilty of willfully violating workplace safety rules in the death of Blake Lane. Lane, just 20 years old, was on his second day on the job when he was electrocuted on a high-power-line steel tower. The jury took more than four hours to render a split verdict for L.E. Myers. L.E. Myers faced a maximum sentence of five years' probation and a $500,000 fine for the misdemeanor charge.

    Following the Golab and similar cases, in 1989–1990, California enacted the Corporate Criminal Liability Act, popularly known as the Be a Manager, Go to Jail act. This law subjects managers of corporations and limited liability companies to criminal liability for failing to disclose "concealed hazards." A manager (or executive/ senior manager) of a corporation must notify the Department of Occupational Safety and Health and warn employees in writing immediately if there is imminent risk of "great bodily harm or death." The act imposes fines and jail time on violators.

Whistleblower Program

Your business may face legal fines and citations under the federal Whistleblower Program.

OSHA was passed to achieve safer and more healthful workplaces throughout the nation, and the act provides for a wide range of rights for employees and representatives of employees.

To help ensure that employees are, in fact, free to participate in safety and health activities, Section 11(c) of the act prohibits any person from discharging or in any manner discriminating against any employee because he or she has exercised rights under the act.

These rights include complaining to OSHA and seeking an OSHA inspection, participating in an OSHA inspection, and participating or testifying in any proceeding related to an OSHA inspection.

"Discrimination" can include these actions:

- Firing or laying off
- Assigning to undesirable shifts

- Blacklisting

- Demoting

- Denying overtime or promotion

- Disciplining

- Denial of benefits

- Failure to hire or rehire

- Intimidation

- Transferring

- Reassigning work

- Reducing pay or hours

OSHA also administers the whistleblowing provisions of 13 other statutes, protecting employees who report violations of various trucking, airline, nuclear power, pipeline, environmental, and securities laws.

If employees believe their employer has discriminated against them because they exercised their safety and health rights, they are advised to contact their local OSHA office right away. Most discrimination complaints will fall under the act, which gives an employee just 30 days to report the discrimination.

Most organizations have little to worry about in regard to our discussion of moral and ethical issues. The vast majority of employers care for their workers, but there are a few who, based on their actions, have forced legislators to pass laws and standards. Given consistent effort, meaningful communication, and honesty, employers will not find themselves subject to whistleblower actions, faced with criminal prosecution, or accused of perpetuating unfair and unsafe trade practices. As with everything else we've discussed, these are meaningful topics. With consistent analysis and program activities, you will be able to avoid such concerns.

Knowledge of business continuity planning and risk management and a review of ethical issues undoubtedly will assist you in developing more meaningful workplace safety programs. You will accomplish this in part by engendering support from others within your organization and from refining your program development and deployment efforts.

BEST PRACTICES

The checklist that follows recaps the critical elements discussed in this chapter and provides a guide for the analysis and enhancement of your workplace safety efforts. Each "no" answer should serve as an incentive to enhance your program in regard to overall business continuity and risk management considerations.

Threat Assessment and Emergency Planning

_____ *Have you led your company through a threat exposure exercise, and do you know what natural, technological, human or contingent threats your company may be exposed to? (See Selected References and Resources, "Threat Matrix.")*

_____ *Does your workplace safety program contain a section on emergency response and planning?*

_____ *Does your plan include specific response protocols for the identified threats? Where necessary, has appropriate personal protection equipment been identified, obtained, and made available?*

_____ *Have employees and other critical personnel been trained on their role and responsibilities when an emergency arises?*

_____ *Have such roles and responsibilities been practiced or have drills taken place to ensure that each emergency response team member understands his role and responds accordingly?*

_____ *Have backup or replacement personnel been identified for your response team members in the event they are not available during an emergency?*

_____ *Has your company acquired the necessary communication tools and equipment for use in an emergency?*

_____ *Do you or others know how to notify response personnel that an emergency situation exists?*

Crisis Management

_____ *Has your company identified a location to serve as an emergency operations center (EOC) or event management command center?*

_____ *Has your EOC been supplied with the necessary resources, including communication, clerical, food, water, and personal hygiene as well as other specific needs, such as blueprints and maps?*

_____ *Do your planning efforts include practice activation of the EOC to ensure that it is available as needed, that supplies have not been pilfered, and that all infrastructure components (e.g., communication devices) are operational?*

Crisis Communication

_____ *Have you identified those who may communicate with the media, regulatory agency personnel, or outside emergency response teams?*

_____ *Has your company adopted a communications system that is understood by all? That is, do you use codes or code words that may be confusing to some team members?*

_____ *Can you communicate with workers at remote sites?*

_____ *Does your plan include procedures for multiple communication capabilities, including the use of your Web site, for both internal and external constituents?*

Business or Operational Recovery

_____ *Have you identified critical operations that must be brought back on line after an emergency or disaster and identified the time frames for doing so?*

_____ *Have you developed or will you be developing a systematic plan for operational recovery that is focused on your company's critical functions and their restoration within agreed-on time frames?*

_____ *Do you have single or sole source suppliers of goods or services? If so, have you embarked on plans to identify backup providers to your single sources or other alternatives for recovery for those in the sole-source arena?*

Risk Management

_____ *Have you identified exposures to loss for your company's resources and assets within the property, liability, personnel, and financial realms?*

_____ Based on the potential magnitude of loss, are there any operations or activities, where it may be in your best interest to avoid the exposures altogether?

_____ Have you physically or operationally segregated critical resources, personnel, and processes to avoid the total loss of any one critical resource?

_____ Can you support the duplication of resources (e.g., backup copies, cross-trained personnel, mirrored information technology infrastructure) to minimize the potential for a critical resource not being available when needed?

_____ Has the management team conducted analyzed operations that entail significant risk to determine if contractual transfer, such as subcontracting a task, should be implemented?

_____ Are as many adverse outcomes as possible reviewed for contractual risk financing, and has the level for retaining losses (economic losses, deductibles, self insured retentions, etc.) been established and made part of your company's financial planning?

Ethics

_____ Have you established an ethical barometer for your company?

_____ Do you enforce established ethical behavior among all of your management team and employees?

_____ If you are a publicly traded company, have you reviewed all regulatory corporate governance considerations (i.e., Sarbanes-Oxley) and incorporated those into your ethics program and review process?

_____ Have you analyzed the organizations you do business with to determine if they have an active ethics program, participate in groups such as the Fair Trade Federation, and can validate they treat their employees and constituents with dignity and respect?

_____ Do you meet on occasion, such as annually, with outside counsel to ensure that your company is looking at required regulatory mandates, laws, and rules?

_____ Have you made ethics and ethical behavior part of the core values of your company, and have such values been published?

CHAPTER 6

Workers' Compensation and Insurance

This chapter focuses on implementing strategies that lead to success in your workers' compensation and insurance programs. It is not a comprehensive review of workers' compensation and insurance; such details can be obtained through classroom and online instruction; your insurance carrier, third-party administrator, insurance agent, or broker; and industry associations.

WORKERS' COMPENSATION

Workers' compensation programs in the United States are state regulated, with laws determined by each state's legislative body and implemented by a state agency. The programs provide the payment of lost wages, medical treatment, and rehabilitation services to workers suffering from an occupational injury or disease. Workers' compensation statutes have a few common principles and similar categories of benefits; although the details concerning the level of benefits provided and the administrative mechanisms used to deliver the benefits vary dramatically from state to state.

The basic principle of workers' compensation is that benefits are provided to injured workers without regard to fault. Workers are entitled to benefits (paid by the employer) if the injury was a result of their employment, regardless of the cause of injury. Under workers' compensation, employees give up their right to sue (except under a few rare instances), and employers are responsible for specific benefits in accordance with state law.

Workers' compensation insurance coverage is required in all states except Texas, where coverage is optional (except for public entities). In Texas, those employers that opt out of the workers' compensation system can be sued by employees for failure to provide a safe workplace.

Employers can purchase workers' compensation coverage from private insurance companies (mostly through insurance agents and brokers) or state-run workers' compensation agencies, known as state funds. As of this writing, state funds compete with private insurers (competitive funds) in 14 states; in 5 states, the state is the sole provider of workers' compensation insurance. State funds can also function as the insurer of "last resort" for businesses that have difficulty obtaining coverage in the open market.

In certain injury cases, determining the appropriate amount of benefits (to injured workers) can be difficult, because most jurisdictions attempt to calculate a future wage loss for an individual who has a permanent physical condition that is likely to affect future earning capacity. Estimating future wage losses is not an exact science. Depending on the state, the process can (and often does) involve litigation, which many times is resolved through negotiated agreements and the payment of a lump sum to the injured worker.

Furthermore, not all occupational injuries and diseases are paid for under workers' compensation systems. Coverage exceptions in each jurisdiction and differences in compensability rules eliminate some injuries and illnesses that may be work related. Therefore, some injury cases are denied; they may also be litigated and settled with lump-sum payments.

History of Workers' Compensation

Workers' compensation insurance is a twentieth-century social insurance program whose roots can be traced to ancient times. The code of Hammurabi (1750 BCE) provided compensation for injured workers and stated that punitive action would be taken against one who caused another's injury. From the beginning of recorded history, work-related injuries and illnesses have occurred and efforts have been made to deal with the consequences. These efforts gained momentum with the onset of the industrial revolution.

Workers' compensation laws have their modern origins in Europe. The adoption of such laws in the United States, beginning in 1911, has been called a significant event in the nation's history. By 1921, most states had enacted workers' compensation legislation. The last state to enact workers' compensation statutes was Mississippi in 1948.

Workers' compensation laws have undergone minor alterations over time but in substance they represent a social consensus that the burden of industrial injuries should be paid for by the employer.

Under state workers' compensation laws, injured workers receive medical care for their injuries and loss of income, irrespective of fault in their injury; in exchange, workers forfeit their right to sue an employer for damages (unless there are special circumstances surrounding their injury). Workers' compensation is considered a "no-fault" insurance benefit.

How Rates Are Developed

In all states there exists an administrative organization, designated by that state, to perform certain workers' compensation administration functions. In most states that organization is the National Council on Compensation Insurance (NCCI). In a few states a statewide rating bureau serves the same purpose. All of these organizations perform basically similar functions, including:

- Rate-making
- Development and administration of job classifications
- Development and interpretation of rules for policy issuance and cancellation
- Administering the experience rating plan
- Approving policy forms and endorsements

Underwriting

Underwriting involves the selection and pricing of your company's insurance coverage. Typically, underwriting is performed by underwriters working for insurance carriers. Underwriters price insurance policies, and evaluate the facts surrounding each potential policyholder (your business).

In determining proper insurance premiums, underwriters generally use three criteria: (1) your payroll; (2) your underwriter/employer classification; and (3) your experience record, including the number and severity of injuries and illness.

The first element considered is your total annual company payroll in blocks of $100, followed by a review of your industry classification (type of business). Each industry classification is assigned a designated rate (per $100 of payroll). (For example, roofing companies, which naturally have a higher exposure to injuries, will have a different classification from companies consisting of mostly office personnel, who have a lower exposure to injuries.)

The last consideration is what is known in the industry as the "experience modification factor" or "experience mod" or "X-mod," or simply the "mod" (see "Experience Rating" later in this chapter). NCCI or your state's workers' compensation rating bureau determines your company's experience modification factor by comparing your company with other companies in the same industry classification. As part of the analysis, both the frequency and the severity of injuries are used to develop the experience modification factor. The more injuries (frequency) an employer has had in the past, generally, the higher the experience modification factor. Smaller companies may not be experience rated because of their small premium size.

Underwriting Standards

Each insurance carrier has its own set of underwriting standards as to the acceptability to insure a particular business. Underwriting consideration may include:

- Type of business and associated hazards
- Perceived qualifications and experience level of the owner(s) or management of the business
- Financial stability of the business
- Demonstrated interest in loss prevention and safety
- Injury history (usually three to four years prior)
- Wages, benefits, turnover, seasonal business practices

One of your goals should be to *do everything possible to paint a positive picture* of your organization to your insurance agent or broker and underwriter. Having an effective workplace safety program in place is a good start in demonstrating your organization's commitment to the safety and health of your workforce.

Premium Audit

Insurance carriers may perform a premium audit/payroll audit to compute an accurate insurance premium. Types of audits include:

- *Physical audits* (may be required annually on policies with insurance premiums above a state-determined level). Payroll statements may be accepted in lieu of physical audits at the insurance carrier's discretion.

  During physical audits, the auditor works directly from original payroll records, cross-checking them with unemployment, social security reports, or other records.

  Failure to submit payroll reports or to cooperate with a physical audit can result in cancellation of insurance.

- *Payroll statement audits* (a request for payroll is sent to you by the insurance carrier). If the report is not received within the stated time period, a final notice most likely will be sent. In some instances, the insurance company may estimate payroll. Some key points to remember:

  - The owner or the company's CPA/bookkeeper must sign payroll reports

  - Remuneration (payroll) includes, but is not limited to:
    Gross wages
    Salaries
    Commissions
    Bonuses
    Overtime payments
    Market value of gifts
    Vacation
    Holiday and sick payments
    Board and lodging (if designated in the bureau classification)

Experience Rating

Experience rating tailors the cost of insurance to the performance of the individual employer. It compares an employer's past loss record to all members of that same industry classification, and then the workers' compensation "cost" is then adjusted based on that comparison. This rating system allows you, the employer, the opportunity to control insurance costs through effective workplace safety programs.

As mentioned, the NCCI or your state's workers' compensation rating bureau determines your company's experience modification factor by comparing your company with other companies in the same industry classification. Both frequency and severity of injuries are used in the calculation.

Here are some key points to remember about experience modification factor calculations:

- They can be controlled by keeping injuries and illnesses down.
- A period of three policy years of experience is used for the rating, beginning up to four years and nine months prior to the rating date.
- The most recent policy year is omitted (to permit open or late-reported injuries to close or develop more stable reserves).
- Experience rating considers that *injury frequency is a better measure of good (or poor) management than injury severity*, so the weighting used in calculations places greater emphasis on injury frequency:
  - A higher frequency of injuries penalizes an employer more than injury severity.
  - The impact of injury severity is mitigated by a discounting process. For example, 15 injuries producing $50,000 in losses will have a greater impact than one $50,000 injury.

Exhibit 6.1 demonstrates the impact of experience modification factors on the cost of workers' compensation premium. For example, a new business will be given an experience modification factor of 1.0 (100 percent); however, if over time the company has more workplace injuries than other

EXHIBIT 6.1   EXPERIENCE MODIFICATION FACTOR COMPARISONS

Good (credit)	Average	Poor (debit)
75% (.75) (reduction in manual premium)	100% (1.0)	125% (1.25) (increase in manual premium)

businesses doing the same work, it can result in a debit, thus increasing its workers' compensation premium costs. Should the company incur fewer injuries than like businesses, the result may be a credit resulting in lower premium costs.

At the end of the day, the key to managing your workers' compensation premium cost is how successful your workplace safety program is.

Policy Types

For small to medium sized companies, the majority of workers' compensation policies are written on a "guaranteed cost" basis. *Guaranteed cost* means:

- Barring unexpected changes in payrolls or classifications, the final premium will be known ahead of time.
- The premium amount will not fluctuate based on losses in that year.
- The insurance carrier retains the sole responsibility for the payment of all injuries.

As a company gets larger and becomes more sophisticated in controlling losses through prevention efforts, it sometimes considers the assumption of partial liability in order to reduce workers' compensation premiums. This plan type is called *loss-sensitive.* Loss-sensitive plans require a company to assume some of the losses, similar to paying a deductible.

Coverage

Workers' compensation coverage applies to every person or business entity (public or private) that has any person working for them. In most states, any person working for an employer is eligible for benefits, including aliens and minors. Coverage rules vary by state (check with your insurance carrier or agent to verify); however, there are some general exceptions to mandatory coverage:

- Household or domestic labor usually included under homeowner's policy.
- Volunteers of a nonprofit organization, unless specifically included in the policy.
- True independent contractors with valid contracts are considered non-employees.

- All corporate officers/directors rendering actual service for pay are considered employees and automatically covered; however, individual officers/directors may be excluded by choice if they own stock in the corporation. The percentage of ownership that can be excluded varies by state (see "One Alternative to Workers' Compensation" later in this chapter).

- General partners can elect to be excluded from the policy.

- Other exceptions relating to family may be considered.

- As discussed earlier, workers' compensation insurance coverage is required in all states except Texas, where workers' compensation coverage is optional (except for public entities).

What Are Work-Related Injuries, Illnesses, and Benefits?

Over the past 75 years, case law and legislative revisions in each state have defined and clarified which medical conditions and under what circumstances injuries and diseases are considered occupationally related and therefore compensable under the workers' compensation statute within each state. The definition of injury and illness work-relatedness differs by state; however, in general:

Covered (work-related):

- Injuries arising out of and occurring in the course of employment
- Diseases arising out of the employment
- Acute or cumulative injuries

Not Covered (non–work-related):

- Injuries caused by the intoxication of the injured employee, where the intoxication is the primary cause of the injury
- Intentionally self-inflicted injuries or suicide (with the exception of police officers in certain states)
- Injuries to the initial physical aggressor in an altercation
- Injuries arising out of voluntary participation in off-duty recreational, social, or athletic activities that are not part of the employee's work-related duties

Benefits

When covered employees suffer a work-related injury or disease, they are entitled to specific medical, disability, vocational, and death benefits itemized in each state. Although there are separate laws for each state and separate laws for federal employees, railroad workers, seafarers, and longshore and shipyard workers, the general benefits available are similar and include:

- Payment of reasonable and necessary medical treatment to cure and relieve the employee from the physical effects of the injury (*medical expenses*)
- Replacement of wages lost because of the injury

    - Temporary disability, which includes both temporary total disability and temporary partial disability
    - Permanent disability, which includes both permanent partial disability and permanent total disability

- Vocational rehabilitation benefits (or monetary equivalent) for workers whose injury led to permanent physical limitations that prevent them from returning to the occupation they had at the time of their injury
- Death benefits to the surviving spouse and to any minor children (with caps on the amount of benefit)
- Funeral and dependency benefits if a worker dies from an occupationally related injury or disease

Disputes and Settlements

Disputes or disagreements over benefits can occur at any time in the life of a workers' compensation injury case and can arise over any issue. The most commonly disputed issues are:

- Initial compensability (whether the injury or disease is work-related)
- Whether the current disability is related to the work-related injury or disease
- Whether and when the employee can return to work
- Extent of physical limitations and whether they are temporary or permanent

- Extent of permanent partial disability or entitlement to ongoing wage-loss benefits
- Entitlement to permanent total disability benefits and, if entitled, for how much and how long

With a few exceptions, most jurisdictions allow settlements of workers' compensation cases. These settlements may also be termed *compromise-and-release* agreements, commutations, or washouts. In most instances, the employer (working with the insurance carrier) will attempt to settle all future benefits, including medical payments, in jurisdictions that allow this. There are times where a compromise-and-release agreement may not be a smart business decision, so before entering into such agreements, talk with your insurance carrier and insurance agent or broker.

Recovery Opportunities

Some workers' compensation statutes contain the opportunity to reduce costs through a number of methods. These methods include third-party recoveries, state and federal statutes, and apportionments. Broadly speaking, these opportunities might include:

- Reducing reserves
- Subrogation
- Disability (both state and federal)
- Second injury funds
- Apportionment

Should an employee suffer a significant workers' compensation injury, be sure to talk with your insurance carrier and agent or broker about recovery opportunities. By far, managing injury case reserves can be an effective recovery opportunity.

Workers' Compensation Fraud

Recent publicity about workers' compensation fraud shows a lot of misunderstanding about what fraud is. An employee, employer, medical provider, attorney, or other party can commit fraud. For a successful prosecution, the false representation must be knowingly made with intent to

deceive, and the false representation must be material and make a difference in what happens. The purpose of the false representation must be to
obtain or deny compensation benefits. In the workers' compensation system, many questionable and even abusive practices fall short of the legal
definition of workers' compensation fraud. These cases can't be prosecuted
successfully under the many antifraud laws.

Although employees should know that you are serious about preventing
fraud, it is a mistake to treat every workers' compensation injury case as
fraudulent. This creates unnecessary litigation, which increases injury case
costs, which increases your costs through higher premiums. And it's bad
for the morale of your employees. That said, if you suspect genuine fraud,
report it to your insurance company, third-party administrator, and insurance agent or broker right away. Many insurance carriers have a Special
Investigations Unit (SIU) that investigates fraud. Cases with enough evidence of wrongdoing may be turned over to state insurance fraud units and
local district attorneys for further investigation and prosecution.

There are often "red flags" that may be indicators of fraud but do not
necessarily mean that fraud exists. For example:

General

- Unwitnessed incident
- Vague details or rumors at workplace that incident is staged/
  illegitimate
- Injury complaints inconsistent with facts of incident
- Friday afternoon or Monday morning injury, especially if Friday
  injury is not reported until Monday
- Incident occurring in area not normally frequented by employee
- Incident not of type associated with job duties
- Incident unreported to employer by employee
- Multiple versions of incident

Workers' Compensation Injury Case (Claims) Form

- Contains contradictory or irreconcilable information
- Submitted by questionable/high-volume attorney or medical facility

- Delayed completion (greater than 24 hours after incident)
- Alleges continuous trauma or multiple body parts
- Multiple injuries

Injured Worker

- Reportedly employed elsewhere or engaged in activity inconsistent with injury
- Has a history of previous injuries
- Questionable identity/residence/phone (during phone conversations background noises are inconsistent with residence)
- Retiring, on probation, involved in labor dispute, disgruntled, poor job performer, or subject to disciplinary action
- Never at home, does not answer phone, avoids use of e-mail and regular mail
- Overly familiar with workers' compensation system or terminology
- Unexplained/excessive time off prior to the stated injury, recovery time exceeds medical protocol guidelines
- Inquires about quick settlement
- Protests about modified position or returning to work

General Premium/Policy (Red Flags that Underwriters Watch for in Businesses)

- Unusual change of ownership
- Severe fluctuations in reported payroll
- Policyholder (business) refuses safety inspection, investigation, or audit
- Employer not concerned with safety procedures
- Work site differs from that listed on the policy
- A pattern where the losses have considerably exceeded the premium
- Equipment and vehicles in yard without operator/mechanic exposure
- Payroll not consistent with number of employees

Minimizing the Cost of Injuries

Before an Injury

Establishing an effective workplace safety program will serve as a key benefit in the management of workers' compensation costs and employee injuries. In addition to your workplace safety program:

- Maintain a consistent hiring policy.

- Use employment applications and check prior employers, educational background, and references. (It is illegal to ask applicants about prior workers' compensation injuries.)

- Educate employees on workers' compensation (rather than leaving that up to television commercials, bus stop signs, billboards, and attorneys).

- Differentiate for your employees about health insurance, state disability, unemployment, and workers' compensation.

- Communicate with all parties involved.

- Develop a "gatekeeper" process where all injuries are funneled and reviewed.

After an Injury

Given the billions of dollars that employers spend annually on workers' compensation, it is surprising that so little is known about injured or ill workers' expectations, perceptions, and experiences within the workers' compensation process. Beginning in 1997, Intracorp, in partnership with The Gallup Organization, studied injured workers' experiences and perceptions.[1]

The Intracorp study focused on the experiences and perceptions of injured workers. The results may be unexpected and even, at times, contradictory to information that employers report. The survey results were presented according to the stages of a workers' compensation injury or illness: preinjury, time of injury, treatment, recovery, and return to work.

Several surprisingly simple employer initiatives can significantly affect workers' compensation program outcomes. According to the study, prior communication and post-injury demonstrations of concern and caring drove higher levels of injured worker satisfaction, reduced time lost from work, and reduced attorney involvement—all factors that contribute to lower insurance program costs. The good news is that, with a focused strategy, employers can easily address these factors and improve their workers' compensation program results. Some of these initiatives include:

- Stay connected with injured workers (communication counts).
- Show you care.
- Treat people the way you would want to be treated if you were injured.
- Get help/medical care quickly for injured.
- Send get well cards (signed by staff).
- Send flowers or other means of recognition.
- Make visits/calls.
- Demonstrate understanding, caring behavior.
- Discuss job security ("You will not lose your job over this").

Additional data suggest that workers' compensation costs can be further minimized in these ways:

- Establish a network of medical providers.
- Exercise control and use an occupational/industrial medical provider. (In some states, this may be designated by the carrier.)
- Communicate this information (workers' compensation benefits and guidelines) to employees.
- Conduct incident investigations.
- Pursue a return-to-work plan and modified duty programs.
- Communicate with the injured worker on a regular basis, and help smooth out any problems with insurance-related issues.

In summary, you should make efforts to integrate your workplace safety program and workers' compensation programs, and:

- Let employees know that you care—talk to them after they have been injured and let them know you'll do everything possible to ensure that the workers' compensation journey is a smooth one.
- Work closely with workers' compensation providers and follow up on the status of injury cases frequently.

- Provide an avenue for injured workers to return to work as soon as possible.

- Investigate injuries and resolve unsafe actions or conditions as rapidly as possible. Doing this reduces the chance of similar injuries and validates to all other employees your sincerity toward controlling them in the future.

Immediate Reporting and Investigation

Your company will greatly benefit from programs that not only require prompt workers' compensation injury reporting but have mechanisms to ensure such reporting. In some cases, injuries and illnesses are obvious; in others, employees may just feel discomfort, and delay reporting. Employees should be encouraged and trained to notify supervisors or management as soon as they experience discomfort or sustain an injury. In some cases, they may be injured and need help. In others, it may be appropriate to wait. It has been shown that prompt medical care and reporting helps to ultimately control workers' compensation injury costs.

As shown in Exhibit 6.2, in a recent Hartford study, injuries reported within two weeks of injury were 18 percent more expensive than those reported within one week. Injuries reported within three weeks were 29 percent more expensive than those reported within one week. Similarly,

EXHIBIT 6.2   WORKERS' COMPENSATION REPORTING SPEED AND INJURY COSTS

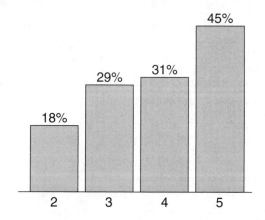

Source: Hartford Insurance, 2000.

injuries reported at four weeks were 31 percent more expensive, and injuries reported at five weeks were 45 percent more costly.[2]

Reporting injuries as soon as they are known or suspected also allows you, as a company, to conduct an incident investigation and resolve unsafe acts or unsafe conditions, reducing the potential for similar events to occur in the future.

Developing a Formal Return-to-Work Program

The total cost of an injury is comprised of medical costs, lost wages, and rehabilitation costs. (Costs also include a loading for administrative fees and potential profit for a workers' compensation carrier.) If you can provide alternatives for an employee who is injured to return to work, you can control or limit costs in most of your injury cost categories.

Your company's role in providing *light, modified,* or *alternate* work rests in part with ensuring that the injured worker does not take on tasks that compound the existing injury or serve to create new injury exposures. (The latter also applies to not exposing co-workers to possible new hazards due to an employee returning to modified duty.)

- Light-duty assignments generally imply that an employee conducts normal tasks, but a lighter rate or intensity or with lighter (less) physical demands.

- Modified work assignments are those that injured employees can take on that require physical and/or administrative modifications to a task or job, or might require adaptive aids.

   In both light and modified assignments, the costs of lost wages are controlled, benefiting current and future costs of workers' compensation costs. Studies have also shown that workers who return to work sooner, rather than later, recover more quickly and benefit from the social structure that the workplace provides.[3]

- Alternate work is just that. If an injured worker can take on an alternate work assignment, the lost-time costs of the injured are controlled.

The decisions for assigning light, modified, or alternate work is made by three parties: you, the injured worker, and the medical provider. The medical provider is the one who determines what type of activities an injured worker may take on and for what period of time.

Some carriers and states provide financial incentives to employers for introducing and managing return-to-work programs. But consider this: If employees do not become injured or ill, they will never have to be considered for the return-to-work program in the first place. There is a much larger financial benefit in achieving that outcome.

As mentioned, staying in touch with injured workers must be a high priority. As described in the Intracorp studies, employees who stay connected to their supervisors and companies while they are convalescing recover more quickly.

Relationships with Medical Providers

Medical providers play an essential role in the success of your workers' compensation program. Here are three helpful hints that will enhance your workers' compensation program efforts:

1. Interview workers' compensation medical providers and determine which one is best for handling occupational injuries and illnesses. Not all medical providers are specialists in the occupational arena.

2. Advise the medical providers by letter that you expect exceptional treatment and that you may want to have the option of paying for first-aid injury cases.

3. Have your medical provider visit your facility and observe operations. During their visit, doctors will get a firsthand glimpse of the exposures leading to injury or illness to your employees. This will assist them in determining whether someone is sent for treatment has a work-related problem or not. Equally important, they will be able to work more closely with you on return-to-work strategies once they have visited your operations. (You might also consider taking a video or sending a DVD of your operations. Such ancillary information can assist medical providers in determining the type and causes of injury as well as appropriate medical treatment. Visual evidence of tasks can be especially helpful in managing injuries from ergonomic risk factors.)

Medical providers will also benefit from being provided copies of material safety data sheets (MSDSs) for chemicals and substances employees work with. These MSDSs should be labeled with any slang terminology that might be used by an employee. Such terms include, for example, *trike* for trichloroethane. The quicker your medical provider can determine what an employee has been exposed to, the quicker and better treatment they are able to provide. Packaging a set of MSDSs for your medical provider is a good approach, as is sending MSDSs when employees go for treatment.

Develop a Good Relationship with Your Insurance Carrier

Tremendous benefits accrue when a company develops solid relationships with a workers' compensation carrier. Most carriers employ, in addition to their claims personnel, a department of outsourced function of professional safety and health staff. Together, claims and safety staff (often referred to as loss control or risk control consultants), may be able to assist you in developing a workers' compensation cost control program. This program includes helping to determine medical providers to choose from, conducting site safety and health surveys, conducting training sessions for supervision and management, and working with you on the design and deployment of return-to-work programs. Be aware, though: Many of these services may be limited through an insurance carrier and may be based on the amount of premium you pay. For many small and midsized companies, such insurance carrier services may not be available.

Workers' compensation insurance carriers have a vested interest in helping you in your efforts to control the frequency and costs associated with injuries. By working together on safety issues, injury cases, and return-to-work strategies, you both will win.

By developing a strong relationship with insurance carriers and medical providers, employers are also able to:

- Reduce the inclusion of non–workers' compensation injuries into the system (such as work-related injuries that are really health cases), which can directly impact the future cost of coverage
- More rapidly detect fraudulent cases and restrict their entry into the workers' compensation system

INSURANCE AGENTS AND BROKERS

Like bankers, CPAs, and attorneys, professional insurance agents and brokers are of vital importance to your company. In most cases, they are your direct link, spokesperson, and "marketing representative" to the commercial insurance market. And part of their job is to represent you in your efforts to secure the best value and price for your insurance needs. They should be knowledgeable about your business and the insurance programs necessary to protect it. Whether it's conducting an insurance contract review (for insurance and indemnity reasons), due diligence assistance, recommending risk and safety management services, helping settle an injury case, or securing the best insurance market for your business, we recommend that you choose your agent first—meaning that you make every effort to refrain from "price shopping" and "getting quotes" from different agents and brokers (each year) to purchase commercial insurance. Would you price shop and look for a new banker, attorney, or CPA each year?

Businesses that establish long-term relationships with a good insurance agent or broker are more stable and loyal in the eyes of insurance carriers and underwriters. And a good agent or broker gains the respect of insurance carriers and underwriters, lending to a more favorable view of your company.

Most people have their first contact with an insurance company through an insurance agent or broker (called a *producer* in the industry). As we discussed, agents and brokers help businesses select insurance policies that provide the best protection for their workforce and business.

Insurance agents who work exclusively for one insurance company are sometimes called captive agents. Independent insurance agents or brokers represent several companies and place insurance policies for their clients with the company that offers the best value, rate, and coverage. Types of insurance agents include:

- Independent agents

    - Does business with and represents a wide variety of regional and national insurance companies
    - Works with you to select the carrier they feel offers the best protection, price, and service tailored to customer needs
- Brokers

    - Usually work for large, nationwide, or international brokerage firms
- Direct writers (only write insurance for the carrier they are employed by)

    - Cannot market business to other insurance companies

- Combination agents (some carriers allow their direct agents to work with other carriers)

Today, there is very little perceived difference between the independent agent and broker—both are focused on representing you, the business owner.

In all cases, agents and brokers "market" your business to underwriters (of insurance carriers), prepare applications, maintain records, service clients, and help prevent losses. They can also help a business with injury case management and workplace safety and health (through its affiliations or in-house staff). A good agent or broker also provides advice on ways in which clients can minimize risk.

Insurance agents and brokers may sell one or more types of insurance, such as property and casualty, life, health, disability, and long-term care. An agent that sells commercial insurance provides coverage such as:

- Workers' compensation
- Property, auto, and general liability
- Products liability
- Employment practices liability
- Professional liability and errors and omissions
- Directors and officers
- Health benefits

The growth of the Internet is gradually altering the relationship between agents, brokers and their clients. Increasingly, companies can obtain insurance quotes from a company's Web site and then contact the company directly to discuss and purchase policies. However, as we stated previously, and for most companies, we recommend that you work with a professional insurance agent or broker.

Insurance agents and brokers must obtain a license in the states where they plan to do business. In most states, licenses are issued only to applicants who complete specified prelicensing courses and who pass state examinations covering insurance fundamentals and state insurance laws.

Commissions and Compensation

Most agents and brokers are paid by commission only; however, workers who are employees of an agency, broker, or insurance carrier may be paid in one of three ways: salary only, salary plus commission, or salary plus bonus.

In general, commissions are the most common form of compensation. The amount of the commission depends on the type and amount of insurance sold and sometimes on whether the transaction is a new policy or a renewal.

When commissions are the form of compensation, agents and brokers are compensated by the insuring company as a percentage of the premium. Commissions can vary between 1% to 20%, depending on the type of insurance coverage and premium amount.

Some agents and brokers prefer a flat fee for their services rather than a commission.

Agent/Broker of Record Letter

An agent/broker of record letter is a document that you, the business owner, completes to appoint a new broker. Most agents and brokers have a standard letter/language you can use to place on your letterhead. The letter usually is addressed to the insurance carrier with a copy to both the incumbent and newly appointed broker. The agent/broker of record letter essentially indicates that a designated broker can/will handle certain insurance contracts for you.

ONE ALTERNATIVE TO WORKERS' COMPENSATION

A study conducted by the National Center for Employee Ownership (NCEO) found that employee-owned companies "have lower workers' compensation insurance rates" than comparable nonemployee-owned companies. The study compared the experience ratings of employee-owned companies to nonemployee-owned companies in similar industries.[4]

From 1998 to 2002, according to the National Association of Insurance Commissioners (NAIC), the California workers' compensation insurance market generated losses in excess of $15 billion. These devastating losses drove 26 insurers from the California market in the same period. Insurers went bankrupt, were seized, or left the California market.[5]

There are few legitimate alternatives to workers' compensation coverage in the United States; however, based on the business insurance climate created in California from 1998 to 2003, a creative approach was developed around the concept of providing a 24-hour/7-day-a-week health, life, and disability benefit to companies with extremely high insurance rates.

Enter Gene Magre, a California contractor, entrepreneur, and owner of an employee-owned company called Historic Ranch Restorations. After years of skyrocketing workers' compensation insurance rates, instability in the insurance market, and few choices for workers' compensation coverage, Magre restructured his company to help him save thousands of dollars in workers' compensation costs. How did he do it?

All California employers (as in other states) must provide workers' compensation benefits to their employees (under California Labor Code Section 3700). If a business employs one or more employees, then it must satisfy the requirement of the law. However, there are exclusions:

- A business owner (sole proprietor) may exclude him- or herself.
- Executive officers and directors who fully own a corporation may elect to be excluded from workers' compensation benefits.

When Historic Ranch Restorations saw savings by making its employees the company's owners, Magre decided he could help other companies do the same thing. That's when he founded ConAPA, a membership-based association of small to mediumsized construction contractors.

Magre's vision was to merge health, disability, life, and dental benefit packages for employee-owned companies. (The ConAPA program relies on the state labor code's allowance for owners of closely held corporations to be excluded from the workers' compensation coverage requirement, also found in other states besides California.) The ConAPA model has requirements involving the number of hours an employee must work before becoming an owner and other guidelines, including having an effective workplace safety program in place. According to Magre, "Joining forces with some of the largest insurance carriers in the country, the ConAPA program is designed to provide health, disability, and life insurance coverage 24 hours a day, 7 days a week regardless of any preexisting conditions."[6]

In 2005, and according to ConAPA, contractors, for example, pay approximately $2,040 monthly in workers' compensation premiums to insure a 25-year-old carpenter earning $20 per hour. If that employee becomes a shareholder and is therefore excluded from the workers' compensation requirement, the company's monthly life, disability and healthcare cost for the carpenter would be $274. For that employee alone, the savings is $1,766 per month or $21,192 annually. In addition, the individual enjoys full coverage 168 hours per week instead of just 40 hours per week as covered by workers' compensation.

Gene's approach is grounded in the belief that employee ownership improves business operations and employee relations, creates safer workplaces, and reduces work-related and on-the-job injuries. The bottom line is that employee ownership can provide a win–win benefit for all of the company's owners.[7]

Many states allow ownership exemptions for workers' compensation. Check with your state insurance department, or www.workplacesafetynow .com for more information about workers' compensation regulations.

BEYOND WORKERS' COMPENSATION

In 1941, President Franklin Roosevelt called on every citizen to lead a "concerted and intensified campaign against accidents." As a direct result of FDR's national call and in the ensuing years, business professionals, union leaders, and working people from every job description rallied to establish effective ways to prevent injuries and illness in the workplace. And we have been successful: Injury rates have been decreasing ever since.

Important as it is to prevent workplace injuries and illness, we must recognize that disease and away-from-work injuries are harming our workforce. For example, the Centers for Disease Control and Prevention reports that:[8]

- Approximately 100,000 people are killed in accidents, yet less than 10 percent of those deaths occurred in the workplace.
- 30 percent of Americans die from cancer.
- Heart disease and stroke are the nation's first leading cause of death, accounting for nearly 40 percent of all early deaths.
- Almost 90 percent of middle-age Americans will develop high blood pressure in their lifetime. And nearly 70 percent of those with high blood pressure will not have it under control.
- Ten million Americans are disabled as a result of stroke and heart disease.

- In a recent year, workplace injury costs were $50 billion—a steep number, but cardiovascular disease alone is estimated at $351 billion.

- Heart disease is a leading cause of premature, permanent disability in the U.S. labor force.

Perhaps the single most critical business threat today is the unhealthiness of our workforce. Should the business community be leading a determined campaign to support healthier lifestyles among workers?

CHAPTER 7

Greatest Lessons Learned in Achieving Safety Success

At the end of the day, you bet on people, not strategies.
—LARRY BOSSIDY, Former CEO, AlliedSignal

For a number of years, we were curious what the current generation of safety professionals, business owners, and front-line supervisors might say is their greatest lesson(s) learned about achieving safety success. This chapter identifies those lessons learned and explores the makings of highly successful safety programs.

CREATING A SAFETY CULTURE

Developing strong safety cultures has the single greatest impact on injury reduction of any process. For this reason, developing a safety culture should be a top priority for all businesses.

What Is Safety Culture?[1]

Safety cultures consist of shared beliefs, practices, and attitudes that exist at an establishment. *Culture* is the atmosphere created by those beliefs, attitudes, and so forth, that shape our behavior. An organization's safety culture is the result of a number of factors, such as:

- Management and employee norms, assumptions, and beliefs
- Management and employee attitudes

- Values, myths, and stories
- Policies and procedures
- Supervisor priorities, responsibilities, and accountability
- Production and bottom-line pressures versus quality issues
- Action or lack of action to correct unsafe behaviors
- Employee training and motivation
- Employee involvement or buy-in

In a strong safety culture, everyone feels responsible for safety and pursues it on a daily basis; employees go beyond the call of duty to identify unsafe conditions and behaviors and intervene to correct them. For instance, in a strong safety culture, any worker would feel comfortable reminding the plant manager or owner to wear safety glasses. This type of behavior would not be viewed as forward or overzealous but would be valued by the organization. Likewise co-workers routinely look out for one another and point out unsafe actions and conditions to each other.

A company with a strong safety culture typically experiences few at-risk behaviors; consequently, it also experiences low injury rates, low turnover, low absenteeism, and high productivity. Such companies usually are extremely safety successful because they excel in all aspects of business.

Creating a safety culture takes time and is frequently a multiyear process. It generally consists of a series of continuous process improvement steps, where employer and employee safety commitment is an integral part of daily operations.

A company just beginning to develop a safety culture usually starts with a small level of safety awareness, such as safety posters and warning signs. As more time and commitment are devoted, a company will begin to address physical hazards and may develop safety recognition programs, create safety committees, and start incentive programs (based on processes, not outcomes).

Your support of a safety culture often results in acquiring a clear commitment to safety, which may translate to company-sponsored advanced safety training for a supervisor (e.g., the OSHA 30 Hour Course, or the Certified Occupational Safety Specialist [COSS] program), hiring a part-time safety professional, and providing resources for incident investigations and safety training.

Further progress toward a true safety culture uses accountability systems.

These systems establish safety goals, measure safety activities, and may charge costs back to areas that incur them. Ultimately, safety becomes everyone's responsibility, not just the responsibility of management and ownership. Safety becomes a value of the organization and is an integral part of operations. Management and employees are committed to and involved in preventing injuries and illnesses.

Over time the norms and beliefs of the organization shift focus from eliminating hazards to eliminating unsafe actions and building systems that proactively improve safety and health conditions. Employee safety and doing something the right way takes precedence over short-term production pressures. Simultaneously, production does not suffer but is enhanced due to the level of excellence developed within the organization.

Building a Safety Culture[2,3]

Any process that brings all levels within the organization together to work on a common goal that everyone holds in high value will strengthen the organizational culture. Worker safety and health is a unique area that can do this. It is one of the few initiatives that offer significant benefits for the front-line workforce. As a result, worker buy-in can be achieved, enabling the organization to implement change effectively. It is much easier to obtain front-line buy-in for improving worker safety and health than it is to get buy-in for improving quality or increasing profitability. When the needed process improvements are implemented, all three areas (safety, quality, and profitability) typically improve, and a culture is developed that supports continuous improvement in all areas.

Safety Culture Process: Getting Started

These next items represent the major processes and milestones that are needed to implement the safety culture process successfully. Note that the list focuses an organization on the process rather than on individual tasks.

People tend to focus on the accomplishment of tasks, that is, to train everyone on a particular concern or topic (e.g., implement a new procedure for incident investigations). Companies that maintain their focus on the larger process to be followed are far more successful. They can see the forest apart from the trees and thus can make midcourse adjustments as needed. Because they never lose sight of their intended goals, they tend not to get distracted or allow obstacles to interfere with their mission. The process itself will take care of the task implementation and ensure that the appropriate resources are provided and priorities are set.[4, 5]

- *Ownership and management buy-in.* This is the very first step that needs to be accomplished. Owners and managers must be on board. If they are not, safety and health will compete against core business issues such as production and profitability. As companies become more safety successful, organizational barriers, such as fear and lack of trust—issues that typically get in the way of all of the organization's goals—are diminished. Most people place a high personal value on their own safety, and if you are sincere in your approach, employees will view your safety efforts as things that are truly being done for them.

- *Continue building buy-in.* Create an alliance or partnership among management, the union (if one exists), and employees. Spell out a compelling reason for the change to everyone. People have to understand *why* they are being asked to change what they normally do and what success will look like.

- *Identify key personnel to champion the change.* If it's only you, make yourself visible, and articulate the reasons for the changes. The reasons need to be compelling and motivational. People frequently respond when they realize how many of their co-workers or subordinates are being injured (or have the potential for injury).

- *Build trust.* Trust is a critical part of accepting change. Trust will occur as different levels within the organization.

- *Conduct self-assessments/benchmarking.* In order to get where you want to go, it is essential to know where you are starting from. Use self-audit mechanisms, visits to other successful companies, and *safety perception surveys* to measure the strengths and weaknesses of your safety culture.

- *Provide initial training* of management and supervisory staff, union leadership (if present), safety and health committee members, and key employees. This training may include safety and health training, and any needed management, team building, hazard recognition, or communication training. By training these people, you have a core group to draw on as resources. Training also gets key personnel on board with needed changes. In a small company, it is your responsibility to train your people effectively.

- *Establish a steering committee (in larger companies).* A steering committee made up of management, employees, union (if present), and safety staff should be established. This group's purpose is to facilitate, support, and direct the safety culture change processes. To be effective, the group must have the authority to get things done.

- *Develop company safety vision.* The company safety vision should consist of key policies, goals, measures, and strategic and operational plans. These policies provide guidance and serve as a check that can be used to see if the decision being made supports or detracts from the organization's intended safety and health improvement process.

- *Align the organization.* The organization should be aligned by establishing a *shared vision* of safety and health goals and objectives. Ownership and management must support the workplace safety program by providing resources (time, training, and equipment) and holding managers and supervisors accountable for doing the same. The entire management and supervisory staff needs to set the example.

- *Define specific roles.* Define roles and responsibilities for safety and health at all levels of the organization. Safety and health must be viewed as everyone's responsibility—*working safe is not a choice.* Clearly spell out how the organization deals with competing pressures and priorities (i.e., production versus safety and health).

- *Develop a system of accountability.* A system of accountability should be developed for all levels of the organization. Everyone must play by the same rules and be held accountable for their areas of responsibility. The sign of a strong culture is when the individuals hold themselves accountable.

- *Develop measures.* Develop measurable objectives and measure the number of:
  - Hazards reported or corrected
  - Safety walk-arounds
  - Equipment checks
  - Safety meetings conducted

- Employees leading a safety meeting
- Completed job safety analyses
- Pre–start-up reviews

STOP COUNTING INJURIES AS THE ONLY MEASURE OF SAFETY SUCCESS.

Overemphasis on injury rates and using them to drive the system is like counting only "failures." In some companies it can drive injury reporting under the table.

- *Policies for recognition.* If policies are created for recognition (for employees doing the right things), continually reevaluate these policies to ensure their effectiveness and that they do not become entitlement programs.
- *Awareness training and kickoff.* A kickoff celebration can be used to announce "It's a new day," and to seek buy-in for any new procedures and programs. Remember the goal is to create a *shared vision* of safety and health goals and objectives.
- *Implement process changes.* Process changes should be implemented via involvement of management, union (if one is present), and employees.
- *Measure continually.* Performance should be measured continually; communicate results and celebrate successes. Publicizing results is very important to sustaining efforts and keeping everyone motivated. Everyone needs to be updated about what's happening in safety. Everyone needs to have a voice; otherwise, people will be reluctant to buy in to the process. A system can be as simple as using current production meetings to talk about safety, a bulletin board, or a comment box.
- *Ongoing support: Reinforcement.* Reinforcement, feedback, reassessment, midcourse corrections, and ongoing training is vital to sustaining a safety culture.

Employee-Owned Companies and Safety

As discussed in Chapter 6, a study conducted by the National Center for Employee Ownership (NCEO) found that employee-owned companies "have lower workers' compensation insurance rates" than comparable non–employee-owned companies. The California study compared the experience modification ratings of employee-owned companies to non–employee-owned companies in similar industries.

According to some research, giving workers a stake in the company's success can be a foundation for an effective workplace safety program. The employee-owned company model of ConAPA (see Chapter 6) has been shown to improve business operations and human resources functions, create safer workplaces, and reduce work-related and on-the-job injuries.[6] Additional advantages include:

- Improved employee loyalty, motivation, and work quality
- Fewer sick days taken
- Shorter recovery period for injuries
- More efficient job-site work routine
- Better time management
- Reduction of lost and stolen tools, equipment, and materials

Giving employees a stake in equity can be the foundation for a superior way of improving operations, productivity, profitability, and safety; however, just handing out some stock won't deliver those results. It takes more. It requires fostering a company-wide entrepreneurial culture—much like building a company safety culture in non–employee-owned companies— in which the employees are active participants.

Making It Easy for Small to Midsized Companies

Employees of an organization, many times, are the ones who provide solutions to their organization's safety problems; they are an essential ingredient for safety success. It is your job to act as facilitators in this process. Core safety success strategies include:

Cultural Alignment:

- Everyone must be pulling in the same direction.
- There must be consistency between what is said about safety and what is done.
- Safety suggestions must be acknowledged.

Getting to Commitment:

- Start before the date of hire—in the interview process, describe your company's commitment and desire for everyone to work safely.

- At date of hire, have every new employee write out three things he or she will do to remain safe on the job. Review the list annually. By making a commitment, people are pulled quickly in the direction of their goal.

Employee Involvement and Engagement:

- Have employees share their safety ideas and thoughts on video (or in a safety meeting), and incorporate the video as part of your core safety program.

- Create safety posters and paycheck stuffers. Try to refrain from using *canned materials.* Take pictures of employees and use their comments in a poster you create and put on the wall.

- Have all employees participate in the safety process: They conduct new-hire orientations, facility safety walk-arounds, and safety meetings.

- If incentive programs are used, they should be process-based (not outcomes-based). Rewards should be based on safety behavior and actions; not solely on a reduction in injuries or costs.

- Never merely copy a workplace safety program and safety philosophy from another company. What's done somewhere else might not work if it's not part of your underlying culture.

- The more employees you have teaching safety, the closer your company gets to those teachers holding safety as a value.

- Remember the old adage, "To change behavior, reverse the role." For example, our behaviors and actions change when we move from learner to teacher or from single person to parent.

Management Processes:[7]

- Define safety responsibilities for all levels of the organization.
- Develop measures (see previous section).
- Align management and supervisors by establishing a shared vision of safety and health goals.

- Implement a process that holds managers and supervisors accountable (such as performance appraisals) for visibly being involved, setting the proper example, and leading a positive change for safety and health

- Evaluate and rebuild any incentives and disciplinary systems for safety and health, as necessary.

- Ensure the safety committee (if there is one) is functioning appropriately.

- Provide multiple paths for employees to bring forward suggestions, concerns, or problems. Ensure no repercussions. Hold yourself accountable for being responsive.

- Develop a system that tracks and ensures timeliness in hazard correction.

- Ensure reporting of injuries, first-aid cases, and near misses. When safety cultures are first forming, prepare for an initial increase in incidents and a rise in rates. This increase can occur at the start of your safety program (if underreporting previously existed in the organization). The rates will level off, and then decline as system changes take hold.

- Evaluate and rebuild the incident investigation system as necessary to ensure that investigations are timely, complete, and effective. They should get to the root causes and avoid blaming workers and supervisors.

12 GREATEST LESSONS LEARNED ABOUT ACHIEVING SAFETY SUCCESS

In the chapter introduction, we discussed what current safety professionals, business owners, and front-line supervisors might say were their greatest lesson(s) learned about achieving safety success. Participants provided over 60 "greatest lessons learned," which we have narrowed down to 12. Those surveyed included a cross-section of top safety professionals and company managers at safety successful companies.

Much has been written in the past 20 years about methods to improve workplace safety. Perhaps the greatest single lesson learned is that there are many ways to create successful workplace safety programs. Different companies, cultures, and management teams require different approaches to achieving safety success.

In addition to the formal survey, over the past two years, we have polled safety professionals, business owners, managers, supervisors, and employees at various levels, asking them to share their "greatest lessons learned" about protecting themselves and others from injury and illness.

Beyond setting up a core workplace safety program and practicing the basics of safety, this "greatest lessons" list identifies key statements and ideas that can lift workplace safety programs from average to excellent. A number of "lessons" may be absent from this list; we've done the best we can to capture the data and the essence of those we polled. Of course, any such list is a project in constant review and analysis. The 12 lessons learned are:

1. Organizations are run by the cultural rules of the workplace.
2. The mere act of showing people that you're concerned about them usually spurs them on to better job performance and integrity.
3. Supervisors are the preferred source of information.
4. Keep intact the dynamic relationship that exists between employee and supervisor.
5. Say only things that are true and say them with total consistency.
6. Be comfortable with being a source of integrity, vision, and intuition. Seek to be producers, not consumers of these rare commodities.[8]
7. Live the values of being a safe person, privately and publicly.
8. Never take the easy way out.
9. Take responsibility—especially for mistakes.
10. Teaching is at the core of leading.
11. Make and keep commitments to safety and health—your own and that of the people you are responsible for.
12. Have employees make a commitment to safety.

According to a number of safety professionals responding to the survey, these are their greatest lesson(s) learned about safety success:

Julie Gasper, Risk Manager and Safety Professional, McBride Electric

- Don't assume that losses are a part of doing business, and help your employees to see this through education.

- Know your audience—not everyone buys in to the moral obligation approach to protect employees.
- Set the tone when new employees join—with a quality safety orientation program.
- View safety as a value, not a priority.
- Don't expect immediate results.
- Safety success is a team effort.

Terry McSween, Ph.D., Founder and CEO of Quality Safety Edge, and author of *The Values-Based Safety Process: Improving Your Safety Culture With Behavior-Based Safety*

- Clearly define the role of management in supporting safety.
- Build accountability for those roles at every level of the organization.
- Create systems that promote the active involvement and participation of all employees.

Allison Fowler, Biotech Safety Professional and Instructor

- Be patient and flexible.
- It's about working with people and being respectful of their agendas and responsibilities.
- Be honest about your skills—ask for help.
- Learn from your mistakes.
- Volunteer and give back to the community.
- Stay in close contact with your networking group.
- Teach and be active in industry-specific organizations.
- Be humble and show respect.

Elise Fischer, Safety and Health Manager, Cox Communications, Orange County

- Listen.
- Give what others want first.
- Take every opportunity to put safety out there in a positive, proactive, and visible way.

- Don't create a separate safety bureaucracy—pair safety with other ongoing events, and so forth.
- Use a reward system such that everyone can earn a reward, not just a few, and then keep it simple.
- Use a wellness approach to safety.
- Express safety as a caring profession.
- Give everyone else the credit and say thank you constantly.

Tom Drake, President, The Drake Group

- Master the essential skills of safety leadership.
- Practice integrity at all times.
- Communicate effectively.
- View activities as processes.

Rick Pollock, President of Comprehensive Loss Management, Inc. and creator of *Blueprints for Safety*

- We're dealing with well-meaning adults who want to do the right thing.
- You can never communicate enough.
- Safety is due to the state of mind of the individual—at the time of the occurrence.
- Multiple factors make up a good safety program.
- Meaningful reward systems work.

Rick Sanchez, Safety and Health Professional and Consultant

- Learn from your mistakes.
- Have the courage to do the right thing.

Aubrey C. Daniels, Founder and Chairman of Aubrey Daniels International and author of *Bringing out the Best in People* and *Measure of a Leader,* among other titles

- Don't underestimate/undervalue positive reinforcement in the development of a safety culture.

- Behavioral technology properly understood and applied works to produce high-performance cultures.

Phyllis Simmons, Founder of Creative Safety Designs

- Managers must walk the talk—show that you care.
- Safety education, building employee relations, and leadership are the building blocks.
- Take care of your employees and safety will follow.

Summarizing a few other pertinent comments:

- Show genuine care and concern for the workforce—seek their well-being first.
- Safety is about the management of hazards.
- Quality of leadership defines the safety climate and organizational culture.
- Strategic leadership is the most important factor.
- This is a people business—safety's not just about rules.

Epilogue

As we suggested at the beginning of this book, without business owners and management leading the safety charge, undertaking specific safety and health measures and the recognition that employees need to be involved in the workplace safety process at all times, the challenges will not abate.

We have attempted to attack those challenges in ways that are not complicated but can easily be embedded in your current business management activities. And we hope that we have shown you ways to handle safety and ensure your company builds safety into its core values, mission, and goals.

We began with a discussion of workplace safety, why it's important, and what the core competencies are to being successful. We covered the relationship of injuries and illnesses to regulatory mandates, financial management, as well as your short- and long-term business goals. And we surveyed top safety professionals and managers at successful companies, learning from them their most treasured lessons about keeping people safe.

As practicing safety professionals, teachers, and business managers, we have learned many safety lessons over our combined years of experience. Foremost among them is that to achieve any workplace safety successes, a first step has to be taken. Whether an audit or best practices review, a foundation must be constructed and plans drafted. The more your safety efforts truly relate to what your employees do and the specific hazards they face, the better outcomes you will experience. We also have learned that safety efforts are never a straight line; they are rather, a journey whose starting point you will visit more than once.

Each of us has a responsibility to make every effort to create a safe workplace for our employees, co-workers, and associates. We're confident that with some effort, teamwork and critical thinking, your safety journey will be successful.

Notes

Chapter 3

1. Occupational Safety and Health Administration (OSHA), *Small Business Handbook*, (Washington, DC: U.S. Government Printing Office, 2005).

Chapter 4

1. Kate Montgomery, *End Your Carpal Tunnel Pain Without Surgery* (Boulder, CO: Sports Touch Publishing, 2004), and Anthony Carey, *The Pain-Free Program* (Hoboken, NJ: John Wiley & Sons, 2005).
2. U.S. Department of Health and Human Services, "Musculoskeletal Disorders and Workplace Factors: A Critical Review of Epidemiological Evidence for Work-Related Musculoskeletal Disorders of the Neck, Upper Extremity, and Low Back," July 1997.
3. NETS (Network of Employers for Traffic Safety), OSHA, and NHTSA (National Highway Traffic Safety Administration) joint publication, "Guidelines for Employers to Reduce Motor Vehicle Crashes."
4. ASIS International, Alexandria, VA 2003.
5. http://travel.state.gov/travel.
6. Bruce Hoffman, *Inside Terrorism* (New York: Columbia University Press, 1998).

Chapter 5

1. Knight, Rory F. and Deborah Petty, "The Impact of Catastrophes on Shareholder Value", The Oxford Executive Research Briefings, Oxford University, 1996.
2. Hopwood, Daniel G. and Bob McAlister, "Business Continuity and Crisis Management: Initial Emergency Response Efforts Are The Key To Success," *The San Diego Daily Transcript*, November 13, 2001, Vol. 16, No. 227
3. Hopwood, Daniel G. and Bob McAlister, "Business Continuity and Crisis Management: Crisis Management and Communications as the Bridge to Recovery," *The San Diego Daily Transcript*, November 20, 2001, Vol. 16, No. 237.
4. See http://training.fema.gov/EMIweb for additional information.
5. George Head and Stephen Horn, *Essentials of Risk Management,* vol. 1 (Malvern, PA: Insurance Institutes of America, 1997).
6. Ibid.
7. Ibid.

Chapter 6

1. Intracorp, *A Study of Injured Workers and Their Experiences with the Workers' Compensation System*, (Philadelphia, PA: 1997).
2. The Hartford Financial Services Group, *The High Cost of Delays: Findings on a Lag-Time Study*, (Hartford, CT: 2000).
3. Juliann Sum, Esq., M.S. in consultation with Laura Stock, M.P.H., *Navigating the California Workers' Compensation System: The Injured Worker's Experience An Evaluation of Services to Inform and Assist Injured Workers in California*, (Berkeley, CA: Prepared for the Commission on Health and Safety and Workers' Compensation, By the Labor Occupational Health Program, University of California at Berkeley 1996).
4. Camille Currier & Steve Thompson, *A Shareholder Solution to Workers' Compensation in California*, (Leading Companies Online Magazine, July 2005, La Jolla, CA: Beyster Institute, web link: http://www.beysterinstitute.org/includes/cfbin/output/article_slot_view.cfm?ID =670726).
5. Ibid.
6. Ibid.
7. ConAPA, www.conapa.net.
8. Centers for Disease Control and Prevention, *Healthy People 2010*, (Hyattsville, MD: U.S. Department of Health and Human Services, National Center for Health Statistics 2000, www.cdc.gov).

Chapter 7

1. Occupational Safety and Health Administration (OSHA), *Safety and Health Management Systems eTool, Module 4, Fact Sheets: Creating a Safety Culture*, (Washington, DC: U.S. Government Printing Office, 2005).
2. Ibid.
3. Leadership—the Driver for Safety and Health, Safety and Health Programs Assistance Training: Achieving Excellence. University of Alabama, March 10, 1996.
4. See note 1.
5. See note 3.
6. Camille Currier & Steve Thompson, *A Shareholder Solution to Workers' Compensation in California*, (Leading Companies Online Magazine, July 2005, La Jolla, CA: Beyster Institute, web link: http://www.beysterinstitute.org/includes/cfbin/output/article_slot _view.cfm?ID=670726).
7. See note 1.
8. Gay Hendricks, Ph.D & Kate Ludeman, Ph.D, *The Corporate Mystic: A Guidebook for Visionaries with Their Feet on the Ground,* (Bantam Books, NY, 1996).

Appendix

Taking Stock Comprehensive Checklist

The Taking Stock Comprehensive Checklist is a reiteration of the points reviewed in chapter 2. In many cases the points have been rephrased.

Who should conduct a review, and how, utilizing this checklist? Several options exist. These include:

- If your organization has a dedicated safety staff person, that person can be assigned the task.

- As the manager or owner of a business, you may need to conduct the analysis.

- Different aspects of this analysis can be divided among various managers, supervisors, or employees. This speeds things up, but the review may end up with biases as not each person will place the same degree of emphasis on each question.

- The review can be undertaken by safety committee members, if you have such a committee or choose to adopt one in the future.

- Some organizations hire an outside professional to conduct the survey; you may find many advantages to this approach.

Regardless of who conducts the assessment, it is important that an initial review be conducted to form a baseline for your organization. Then you must update the analysis regularly to ensure that improvements have been made where necessary, that new processes are investigated for hazards that may not be represented within your workplace safety program, and so forth. This review is not static; it must be a living document.

The checklist has been divided into a number if sections for ease of use.

General Review Questions

_____ *Does your organization's policy statement regarding safety and health management include identification of responsible personnel?*

_____ *Do you conduct regular hazard assessment activities and hazard correction activities?*

_____ *Does your workplace safety program include general rules and regulations or a code of safe practices (specific safety codes and standards) that are operationally and hazard-specific?*

_____ *Can you identify workplace safety communication activities within your plan? Are they documented?*

_____ *Have you developed methods to evaluate, maintain, and improve your safety and health efforts and ensure compliance with your plan?*

_____ *Do your training and education programs specifically support helping employees to understand the codes of safe practices, their roles and responsibilities toward safety, and the ramifications for not following established program requirements (e.g., discipline)?*

_____ *Are you maintaining the tools required to manage safety and your program efforts, including recordkeeping?*

_____ *Are disciplinary actions part of your workplace safety program?*

Management-Oriented Questions

_____ *Have you delineated management's commitment (in writing) to safety and health?*

_____ *Are you ensuring compliance among the workforce regarding codes of safe practice and any other safety and health procedures designed to safeguard their welfare?*

_____ *Have you provided for internal communications that highlight workplace hazards and applicable safety and health procedures?*

_____ *Have you ensured the identification and assessment of hazards that may impact safety and health?*

_____ *Are you conducting incident investigations for all injuries, illnesses, and near misses?*

_____ *Once hazards have been identified through inspection, incident investigations, and other sources, are they corrected and managed in the future?*

_____ *Are you providing for safety and health-related training and education?*

_____ *Do you maintain rigorous records of injury and illness and, if needed, exposure information?*

_____ *Is there an organizational policy statement regarding safety and health and the workplace safety program?*

_____ *Have you/has management made a statement, in writing, regarding a commitment to safety and health?*

_____ *Have the responsibilities of management, supervision, and employees regarding safety and health been clearly defined?*

Compliance-Specific Questions

_____ *Do you instruct workers on the workplace safety program and its intent and content, and the role they play in its success?*

_____ *Do you observe work practices to ensure safe work procedures are being followed? (This requirement can be completed through scheduled inspections or during the normal course of business. As unsafe behaviors are noted, they must be corrected.)*

_____ *Where safety performance by employees is found to be unsafe or unacceptable, do you initiate additional training activities?*

_____ *Are employees disciplined for disregarding safety procedures or consistently working in an unsafe fashion, and is there positive recognition for those who exemplify safe work practices?*

Communication-Focused Questions

_____ *Is there new worker orientation, including a discussion of safety and health policies and procedures?*

_____ *Do you conduct a review of the workplace safety program with employees and ensure that all questions are answered?*

_____ *Do you have training programs, both general and specific hazard-related, in effect?*

_____ *Are there regularly scheduled general safety meetings, as well as those that are issue-specific?*

_____ *Is safety information posted or distributed?*

_____ *Is a system for workers to inform management anonymously about workplace hazards and unsafe acts in effect?*

Hazard Recognition Questions

_____ *Are hazard identification surveys conducted when a program is initiated (sets the baseline)?*

Are surveys conducted:

_____ *When injuries have occurred?*

_____ *When there have been process, equipment, or material changes?*

_____ *When employees have informed you of unsafe acts or conditions?*

_____ *When it is suspected that personal protective equipment needs to be introduced? (This is essential toward ensuring that the proper equipment is obtained.)*

_____ *When required based on a compliance or consultation audit by the applicable OSHA agency?*

Incident Investigation Questions

_____ *Does your firm conduct incident investigations?*

_____ *Are near misses reviewed and investigated?*

_____ *Are those responsible for conducting incident investigations trained in the processes?*

Hazard Resolution Questions

_____ *Do you ensure documentation of hazard correction and control activities?*

_____ *Do you include a section in your workplace safety program to help with such documentation?*

_____ *Do you occasionally audit the documentation and validation efforts of your firm?*

Training Questions

Is training provided:

_____ *When a workplace safety program is first established?*

_____ *To all new workers (although there may be some modifications for construction workers)?*

_____ *To all workers given new job assignments for which training has not previously provided?*

_____ *Whenever new substances, processes, procedures, or equipment are introduced to the workplace and represent a new hazard?*

_____ *Whenever you are made aware of a new or previously unrecognized hazard, including through anonymous reports by employees?*

_____ *To supervisors to familiarize them with the safety and health hazards to which workers under their immediate direction and control may be exposed and to ensure they can provide appropriate training themselves?*

_____ *To all workers with respect to hazards specific to each employee's job assignment?*

_____ *Subsequent to injuries/illnesses?*

Recordkeeping Questions

_____ *Do you maintain and update Form 300, Log of Work-Related Injuries and Illnesses?*

_____ *Do you maintain, update, and post Form 300A, Summary of Work-Related Injuries and Illnesses?*

_____ *Do you regularly complete Form 301, Injuries and Illnesses Incident Report?*

_____ *Do you maintain documents in accordance with mandatory record retention requirements?*

Specific Hazard Review Questions

_____ *Have you conducted a detailed review of specific safety and health concerns?*

_____ *Are there processes, information, and tools available to conduct hazard-specific analyses?*

Ancillary Questions

_____ *Does the safety committee include labor and management representatives?*

_____ *Does the committee meet regularly, but no less often than quarterly?*

_____ *Does the committee prepare and make available to employees written records of the meetings?*

_____ *Are these records retained for agency (e.g., OSHA) review when requested?*

_____ *Do the committee's activities include a review of injuries and illnesses, trends, and related incident investigations?*

_____ *Are recommendations sent to management regarding corrective action and hazard prevention suggestions?*

_____ *Do committee members who have been advised of unsafe acts or conditions bring those concerns to the full committee for review and resolution?*

Activity Calendar Question

_____ *Do you have an activity calendar? (See Selected References and Resources.)*

The goal of an effective workplace safety program is the development of a long-term plan that is successful in protecting people from injury and death, complying with regulations, and controlling the associated financial costs with loss. An effective plan must include methods to:

- Identify and understand all hazards, real and potential.
- Prevent and control hazards so workers are not exposed or so the exposure is minimized.

Selected References and Resources

The following resources (including referenced and endnotes), books, journals and Web sites, have been selected for inclusion in this book. Some of these sources may be found in the endnotes of each chapter, while others are only listed here.

Please note: Resources and supporting materials found in the book may also be downloaded by going to www.workplacesafetynow.com.

BOOKS AND ARTICLES (BY GENERAL SUBJECT)

Crisis Management

Lerbinger, Otto, *The Crisis Manager: Facing Risk and Responsibility*, Lawrence Erlbaum Publishers, Mahwah, NJ, 1997.

Environmental Law

Sullivan, Thomas, F. P., ed., *Environmental Law Handbook*, Government Institutes, Inc., Rockville, MD, 1995.

Health—Occupational

Levy, Barry S. and David Wegman, *Occupational Health, Recognizing and Preventing Work-Related Disease, Third Edition,* Little Brown and Company, Boston, MA, 1995.

Leadership

Gay Hendricks, Ph.D and Kate Ludeman, Ph.D, *The Corporate Mystic: A Guidebook for Visionaries with Their Feet on the Ground*, Bantam Books, NY, 1996.

"Leadership—the Driver for Safety and Health, Safety and Health Programs Assistance Training: Achieving Excellence," University of Alabama, March 10, 1996.

Risk Management

Head, George L., and Stephen Horn II, *Essentials of Risk Management, Volumes 1 and 2, Third Edition*, Insurance Institute of America, Malvern, PA, 1997.

Safety—General

Asfahl, C. Ray, *Industrial Safety and Health Management*, Third Edition, Prentice Hall, Englewood Cliffs, NJ, 1995.

Goetsch, David L., *The Safety and Health Handbook*, Prentice Hall, Upper Saddle River, NJ, 2000.

Goetsch, David L., *Occupational Safety and Health for Technologists, Engineers and Managers, Fourth Edition*, Prentice Hall, Upper Saddle River, NJ 2002.

Kohn, J.P., M.A. Friend and C.A. Winterberger, *Fundamentals of Occupational Safety and Health*, Government Institutes, Inc, Rockville, MD, 1996.

Lack, Richard W. ed., *Essentials of Safety and Health Management*, Lewis Publishers, CRC Press, Boca Raton, FL, 1996.

Occupational Safety and Health Administration (OSHA), *Small Business Handbook*, (Washington, DC: U.S. Government Printing Office, 2005).

Thomen, James R., *Leadership in Safety Management*, John Wiley and Sons, Inc., New York, NY, 1991.

Safety—Shiftwork

Westfall-Lake, Peggy and Glenn N. McBride, *Shiftwork Safety and Performance, A Manual for Managers and Trainers*, Lewis Publishers, Boca Raton, FL 1998.

Safety—Training

Saccaro, Joseph A., *Developing Safety Training Programs, Preventing Accidents and Improving Worker Performance Through Quality Training*, Van Nostrand Reinhold, New York, NY, 1994.

Technological Change

Brown, Marianne and John R. Froines, ed., *Technological Change in the Workplace, Health Impacts for Workers*, The Regents of the University of California, 1993.

Terrorism

Hoffman, Bruce, *Inside Terrorism*, Columbia University Press, New York, NY, 1998.

Violence in the Workplace

Littler, Mendelsohn, Fastiff, Tichy and Mathiason, P.C., *Terror and Violence in the Workplace, Third Edition,* San Francisco, CA, 1996.

Wellness

Centers for Disease Control and Prevention, *Healthy People 2010*, (Hyattsville, MD: U.S. Department of Health and Human Services, National Center for Health Statistics 2000, www.cdc.gov).

Workers' Compensation and Insurance

Camille Currier & Steve Thompson, *A Shareholder Solution to Workers' Compensation in California*, (Leading Companies Online Magazine, July 2005, La Jolla, CA: Beyster Institute, web link: http://www.beysterinstitute.org/includes/cfbin/output/article_slot_view.cfm?ID=670726).

Intracorp, *A Study of Injured Workers and Their Experiences with the Workers' Compensation System,* Philadelphia, PA, 1997.

The Hartford Financial Services Group, *The High Cost of Delays: Findings on a Lag-Time Study*, Hartford, CT, 2000.

Juliann Sum, Esq., M.S. in consultation with Laura Stock, M.P.H., *Navigating the California Workers' Compensation System: The Injured Worker's Experience—An Evaluation of Services to Inform and Assist Injured Workers in California*, (Berkeley, CA: Prepared for the Commission on Health and Safety and Workers' Compensation, By the Labor Occupational Health Program, University of California at Berkeley 1996).

JOURNALS AND MAGAZINES

Disaster Recovery Journal, The DRJ (self-titled) Monthly journal dedicated to Business Continuity Management Issues.

Professional Safety, The Official Publication of the American Society of Safety Engineers.

Risk Management Magazine, The monthly journal of the Risk and Insurance Management Society.

WEB SITES

References within the text to federal OSHA are found within the Fed/OSHA web site at: www.osha.gov.

Employee-Owned Companies

Beyster Institute
www.beysterinstitute.org

ConAPA
www.conapa.net

National Center for Employee Ownership
www.nceo.org

Safety-General

American Association of Safety Councils
www.safetycouncils.org

American National Standards Institute—Safety Related Standards, such as Personal Protective Equipment and Respiratory Protection Equipment
www.ansi.org

American Society of Safety Engineers
www.asse.org

Chemical Safety and Hazard Investigation Board
www.csb.gov

U.S. Department of Labor—Agency that OSHA reports to
www.dol.gov

U.S. Department of Transportation
www.dot.gov

U.S. Environmental Protection Agency
www.epa.gov

U.S. Department of Health and Human Services
www.dhhs.gov

Joint Commission on Accreditation of Hospitals—sections for review include health-care safety and emergency planning
www.jcaho.org

Mine Safety and Health Administration—organization, like OSHA, dedicated to the surface and subsurface mining operations
www.msha.gov

National Fire Protection Association—NFPA Code 1600 focuses on business continuity-related issues
www.nfpa.org

National Institute for Occupational Safety and Health
www.cdc.gov/niosh

National Institute of Standards and Technology—developing standards for business continuity–related issues
www.nist.gov

Occupational Safety and Health Administration
www.osha.gov

Occupational Safety and Health Administration (OSHA), *Safety and Health Management Systems eTool, Module 4, Fact Sheets: Creating a Safety Culture,* (Washington, DC: U.S. Government Printing Office, 2005). (California) OSHA
www.dir.ca.gov/dosh

Pacific Safety Council
www.safetycouncilonline.com

Emergency Preparedness

Federal Emergency Management Agency
www.fema.gov

U.S. Department of Homeland Security
www.dhs.gov/dhspublic

American Red Cross
www.redcross.org

Statistics

Bureau of Labor Statistics (U.S. Department of Labor)—Injuries, Illnesses and Fatalities Statistics
www.bls.gov

Terrorism

Center for Defense and International Security Studies
www.cdiss.org/terror

Foreign Policy Research Institute
www.fpri.org

The Brookings Institution
www.brook.edu

The Terrorism Research Institute
www.terrorism.com

U.S. Department of State—Travel Advisories
www.travel.state.gov

OSHA's Form 300 (Rev. 01/2004)

Log of Work-Related Injuries and Illnesses

Attention: This form contains information relating to employee health and must be used in a manner that protects the confidentiality of employees to the extent possible while the information is being used for occupational safety and health purposes.

U.S. Department of Labor
Occupational Safety and Health Administration

Form approved OMB no. 1218-0176

Year _____

You must record information about every work-related injury or illness that involves loss of consciousness, restricted work activity or job transfer, days away from work, or medical treatment beyond first aid. You must also record significant work-related injuries and illnesses that are diagnosed by a physician or licensed health care professional. You must also record work-related injuries and illnesses that meet any of the specific recording criteria listed in 29 CFR 1904.8 through 1904.12. Feel free to use two lines for a single case if you need to. You must complete an injury and illness incident report (OSHA Form 301) or equivalent form for each injury or illness recorded on this form. If you're not sure whether a case is recordable, call your local OSHA office for help.

Establishment name _____

City _____ State _____

(A) Case No.	(B) Employee's Name	(C) Job Title (e.g., Welder)	(D) Date of injury or onset of illness (mo./day)	(E) Where the event occurred (e.g. Loading dock north end)	(F) Describe injury or illness, parts of body affected, and object/substance that directly injured or made person ill (e.g. Second degree burns on right forearm from acetylene torch)	CHECK ONLY ONE box for each case based on the most serious outcome for that case:				Enter the number of days the injured or ill worker was:		Check the "Injury" column or choose one type of illness:					
						Death (G)	Days away from work (H)	Remained at work		Away From Work (days) (K)	On job transfer or restriction (days) (L)	(M)					
								Job transfer or restriction (I)	Other record-able cases (J)			Injury (1)	Skin Disorder (2)	Respiratory Condition (3)	Poisoning (4)	Hearing Loss (5)	All other illnesses (6)
Page totals						0	0	0	0	0	0	0	0	0	0	0	0

Be sure to transfer these totals to the Summary page (Form 300A) before you post it.

| | Injury (1) | Skin Disorder (2) | Respiratory Condition (3) | Poisoning (4) | Hearing Loss (5) | All other illnesses (6) |

Page 1 of 1

Public reporting burden for this collection of information is estimated to average 14 minutes per response, including time to review the instruction, search and gather the data needed, and complete and review the collection of information. Persons are not required to respond to the collection of information unless it displays a currently valid OMB control number. If you have any comments about these estimates or any aspects of this data collection, contact: US Department of Labor, OSHA Office of Statistics, Room N-3644, 200 Constitution Ave, NW, Washington, DC 20210. Do not send the completed forms to this office.

Identify the person | Describe the case | Classify the case

OSHA's Form 300A (Rev. 01/2004)
Summary of Work-Related Injuries and Illnesses

U.S. Department of Labor
Occupational Safety and Health Administration

Form approved OMB no. 1218-0176

All establishments covered by Part 1904 must complete this Summary page, even if no injuries or illnesses occurred during the year. Remember to review the Log to verify that the entries are complete and accurate before completing this summary.

Using the Log, count the individual entries you made for each category. Then write the totals below, making sure you've added the entries from every page of the log. If you had no cases write "0."

Employees former employees, and their representatives have the right to review the OSHA Form 300 in its entirety. They also have limited access to the OSHA Form 301 or its equivalent. See 29 CFR 1904.35, in OSHA's Recordkeeping rule, for further details on the access provisions for these forms.

Number of Cases

Total number of deaths	Total number of cases with days away from work	Total number of cases with job transfer or restriction	Total number of other recordable cases
0	0	0	0
(G)	(H)	(I)	(J)

Number of Days

Total number of days away from work	Total number of days of job transfer or restriction
0	0
(K)	(L)

Injury and Illness Types

Total number of...
(M)

(1) Injury	0	(4) Poisoning	0
(2) Skin Disorder	0	(5) Hearing Loss	0
(3) Respiratory Condition	0	(6) All Other Illnesses	0

Post this Summary page from February 1 to April 30 of the year following the year covered by the form

Establishment information

Your establishment name _____

Street _____

City _____ State _____ Zip _____

Industry description (e.g., Manufacture of motor truck trailers) _____

Standard Industrial Classification (SIC), if known (e.g., SIC 3715) _____

OR North American Industrial Classification (NAICS), if known (e.g., 336212) _____

Employment information

Annual average number of employees _____

Total hours worked by all employees last year _____

Sign here

Knowingly falsifying this document may result in a fine.

I certify that I have examined this document and that to the best of my knowledge the entries are true, accurate, and complete.

_____ _____
Company executive   Title

_____ _____
Phone   Date

Public reporting burden for this collection of information is estimated to average 50 minutes per response, including time to review the instruction, search and gather the data needed, and complete and review the collection of information. Persons are not required to respond to the collection of information unless it displays a currently valid OMB control number. If you have any comments about these estimates or any aspects of this data collection, contact: US Department of Labor, OSHA Office of Statistics, Room N-3644, 200 Constitution Ave. NW, Washington, DC 20210. Do not send the completed forms to this office.

OSHA's Form 301
Injuries and Illnesses Incident Report

Attention: This form contains information relating to employee health and must be used in a manner that protects the confidentiality of employees to the extent possible while the information is being used for occupational safety and health purposes.

This *Injury and Illness Incident Report* is one of the first forms you must fill out when a recordable work-related injury or illness has occurred. Together with the *Log of Work-Related Injuries and Illnesses* and the accompanying *Summary*, these forms help the employer and OSHA develop a picture of the extent and severity of work-related incidents.

Within 7 calendar days after you receive information that a recordable work-related injury or illness has occurred, you must fill out this form or an equivalent. Some state workers' compensation, insurance, or other reports may be acceptable substitutes. To be considered an equivalent form, any substitute must contain all the information asked for on this form.

According to Public Law 91-596 and 29 CFR 1904, OSHA's recordkeeping rule, you must keep this form on file for 5 years following the year to which it pertains.

If you need additional copies of this form, you may photocopy and use as many as you need.

Completed by _____

Title _____

Phone _____ Date _____

Information about the employee

1) Full Name _____

2) Street _____

   City _____ State _____ Zip _____

3) Date of birth _____

4) Date hired _____

5) ☐ Male
   ☐ Female

Information about the physician or other health care professional

6) Name of physician or other health care professional

   _____

7) If treatment was given away from the worksite, where was it given?

   Facility _____

   Street _____

   City _____ State _____ Zip _____

8) Was employee treated in an emergency room?
   ☐ Yes
   ☐ No

9) Was employee hospitalized overnight as an in-patient?
   ☐ Yes
   ☐ No

Information about the case

10) Case number from the Log _____ *(Transfer the case number from the Log after you record the case.)*

11) Date of injury or illness _____

12) Time employee began work _____ AM/PM

13) Time of event _____ AM/PM ☐ Check if time cannot be determined

14) **What was the employee doing just before the incident occurred?** Describe the activity, as well as the tools, equipment or material the employee was using. Be specific. Examples: "climbing a ladder while carrying roofing materials"; "spraying chlorine from hand sprayer"; "daily computer key-entry."

15) **What happened?** Tell us how the injury occurred. Examples: "When ladder slipped on wet floor, worker fell 20 feet"; "Worker was sprayed with chlorine when gasket broke during replacement"; "Worker developed soreness in wrist over time."

16) **What was the injury or illness?** Tell us the part of the body that was affected and how it was affected; be more specific than "hurt", "pain", or "sore." Examples: "strained back"; "chemical burn, hand"; "carpal tunnel syndrome."

17) **What object or substance directly harmed the employee?** Examples: "concrete floor"; "chlorine"; "radial arm saw." If this question does not apply to the incident, leave it blank.

18) **If the employee died, when did death occur?** Date of death _____

THREAT MATRIX

	Threat	Probability $\times$	Threat Factor[1]	$\times$ Impact	= Relative Weight
Natural	Earthquake				
	Winds				
	Rain				
	Flood				
Human Oriented	Employee Injury				
	Employee Assault				
	Employee Behavior				
	Robbery				
	Vandalism				
	Fire				
	Arson				
	Intruder				
	Weapon-Related				
	Activist				
	Political—Other				
	Terrorism & Bioterrorism				
	Kidnap & Ransom				
	Bomb-Related				
	Visitor Assault				
	Visitor Behavior				
	Visitor Injury				
Technological	Equipment Failure				
	Power Failure				
	System Failure				
	Other Business Interruption				
	Pollution				
	Hazmat-Oriented				
Other	Watercraft				
	Aircraft				
	Vehicle				
	Contingent Threats				

Notes:

(1)**Threat factor:** The sum of the ***Probability factor,*** where 1 = low, 2 = medium and 3 = high, and ***Threat,*** where speed of onset is 0 = slow and 1 = fast; forewarning, where there is forewarning = 0 and no forewarning = 1; duration, where 1 = low, 2 = medium, and 3 = long (add together speed of onset + forewarning + duration); and ***impact,*** where 1 = low, 2 = medium and 3 = high.

Formula: Probability $\times$ Threat Factor $\times$ Impact = Relative Weight

*Relative weight scale created by Ed Devlin, et al. Discussion of scale found in his book, *Business Resumption Planning* (New York, Auerbach Publications,1994).

WORKPLACE SAFETY PROGRAM CHECKUP

If you want to find out how your workplace safety program measures up, take a few minutes to complete this survey. There are no right or wrong answers. This checkup will help identify areas where improvements can be made. Select one answer only per category. Those checked below the bold line require program improvement.

I. Management Leadership and Employee Involvement

A. Clear work-site safety policy	1.	❑ We have a workplace safety policy and all employees accept, can explain, and fully understand it. ❑ We have a workplace safety policy and most employees can explain it. ❑ We have a workplace safety policy and some employees can explain it.
		❑ We have a written (or oral, where appropriate) policy. ❑ We have no policy.
B. Clear goals and objectives are set and communicated	2.	❑ All employees are involved in developing goals and can explain desired results and how results are measured. ❑ Most employees can explain results and measures for achieving them. ❑ Some employees can explain results and measures for achieving them. ❑ We have written (or oral, where appropriate) goals and objectives.
		❑ We have no workplace safety goals and objectives.
C-1. Management leadership	3.	❑ All employees can give examples of management's commitment to workplace safety. ❑ Most employees can give examples of management's active commitment to workplace safety. ❑ Some employees can give examples of management's commitment to workplace safety. ❑ Some evidence exists that top management is committed to workplace safety.
		❑ Workplace safety is not a top management value or concern.
C-2. Management example	4.	❑ All employees recognize that managers in this company always follow the rules and address the safety actions of others. ❑ Managers follow the rules and usually address the safety actions of others. ❑ Managers follow the rules and occasionally address the safety actions of others.
		❑ Managers generally follow basic workplace safety rules. ❑ Managers do not follow basic workplace safety rules.

D. Employee involvement	5.	☐ All employees have ownership of workplace safety and can explain their roles.
		☐ Most employees feel they have a positive impact on identifying and resolving workplace safety issues.
		☐ Some employees feel that they have a positive impact on workplace safety.
		☐ Employees generally feel that their workplace safety input will be considered by supervisors.
		☐ Employee involvement in workplace safety issues is not encouraged nor rewarded.
E. Assigned workplace safety responsibilities	6.	☐ All employees can explain what performance is expected of them.
		☐ Most employees can explain what performance is expected of them.
		☐ Some employees can explain what performance is expected of them.
		☐ Performance expectations are generally spelled out for all employees.
		☐ Specific job responsibilities and performance expectations are generally unknown or hard to find.
F. Authority and resources for workplace safety	7.	☐ All employees believe they have the necessary authority and resources to meet their responsibilities.
		☐ Most employees believe they have the necessary authority and resources to meet their responsibilities.
		☐ Authority and resources are spelled out for all, but there is often a reluctance to use them.
		☐ Authority and resources exist, but most are controlled by supervisors.
		☐ All authority and resources come from supervision and are not delegated.
G. Accountability	8.	☐ Employees are held accountable, and all performance is addressed with appropriate consequences.
		☐ Accountability systems are in place, but consequences used tend to be for negative performance only.
		☐ Employees are generally held accountable, but consequences and rewards do not always follow performance.
		☐ There is some accountability, but it is generally hit or miss.
		☐ There is no effort toward accountability.
H. Program review (quality assurance)	9.	☐ In addition to a comprehensive review, a process is used that drives continuous correction.
		☐ A comprehensive review is conducted at least annually and drives appropriate program modifications.
		☐ A program review is conducted but it doesn't drive all necessary program changes.
		☐ Changes in programs are driven by events such as incidents or near misses.
		☐ There is no program review process.

WORKPLACE SAFETY PROGRAM CHECKUP

Continued

II. Workplace Analysis

A-1. Hazard identification (expert survey)	10.☐ Comprehensive expert surveys are conducted regularly and result in updated hazard inventories.
	☐ Comprehensive expert surveys are conducted periodically and drive appropriate corrective action.
	☐ Comprehensive expert surveys are conducted but corrective actions sometimes lags.
	☐ Expert surveys in response to incidents, complaints, or compliance activity only.
	☐ No comprehensive surveys have been conducted.

A-2. Hazard identification (change analysis)	11.☐ Every planned or new facility, process, material, or equipment is fully reviewed by a competent team, along with affected workers.
	☐ Every planned or new facility, process, material, or equipment is fully reviewed by a competent team.
	☐ High hazard planned or new facility, process, material, or equipment are reviewed
	☐ Hazard reviews of planned or new facilities, processes, materials, or equipment are problem driven.
	☐ No system for hazard review of planned or new facilities exists.

A-3. Hazard identification (job and process analysis)	12.☐ A current hazard analysis exists for all jobs, processes, and material; it is understood by all employees; and employees have had input into the analysis for their jobs.
	☐ A current hazard analysis exists for all jobs, processes, and material, and it is understood by all employees.
	☐ A current hazard analysis exists for all jobs, processes, or phases, and it is understood by many employees.
	☐ A hazard analysis program exists but few are aware of it.
	☐ There is no routine hazard analysis system in place.

A-4. Hazard identification (inspection)	13.☐ Employees and supervisors are trained, conduct routine joint inspections, and all items are corrected.
	☐ Inspections are conducted and all items are corrected; repeat hazards are seldom found.
	☐ Inspections are conducted and most items are corrected, but some hazards are still uncorrected.
	☐ An inspection program exists, but corrective action is not complete; hazards remain uncorrected.
	☐ There is no routine inspection program in place, and many hazards can be found.

B. Hazard reporting system	14.☐ A system exists for hazard reporting, employees feel comfortable using it, and they feel comfortable correcting hazards on their own initiative.
	☐ A system exists for hazard reporting, and employees feel comfortable using it.
	☐ A system exists for hazard reporting, and employees feel they can use it, but the system is slow to respond.
	☐ A system exists for hazard reporting, but employees find it unresponsive or are unclear how to use it.
	☐ There is no hazard reporting system, and/or employees are not comfortable reporting hazards.
C. Incident investigation	15.☐ All loss-producing incidents and near misses are investigated for root cause with effective prevention.
	☐ All OSHA-reportable incidents are investigated and effective prevention is implemented.
	☐ OSHA-reportable incidents are generally investigated; incident cause and/or correction may be inadequate.
	☐ Some investigation of incidents takes place, but root cause is seldom identified and correction is spotty.
	☐ Injuries are either not investigated or investigation is limited to report writing required for compliance.
D. Injury/ illnesses analysis	16.☐ Data trends are fully analyzed and displayed, common causes are communicated, management ensures prevention; and employees are fully aware of trends, causes, and means of prevention.
	☐ Data trends are fully analyzed and displayed, common causes are communicated and management ensures prevention.
	☐ Data are centrally collected and analyzed, and common causes are communicated to supervisors.
	☐ Data are centrally collected and analyzed but not widely communicated for prevention.
	☐ Little or no effort is made to analyze data for trends, causes, and prevention.

III. Hazard Recognition and Resolution

A. Timely and effective hazard control	17.☐ Hazard controls are fully in place, known to and supported by workforce, with concentration on engineering controls and safe work procedures.
	☐ Hazard controls are fully in place with priority to engineering controls, safe work procedures, administrative controls, and personal protective equipment (in that order).
	☐ Hazard controls are fully in place, but there is some reliance on personal protective equipment.
	☐ Hazard controls are generally in place, but there is heavy reliance on personal protective equipment.
	☐ Hazard control is not complete, effective, or appropriate.

WORKPLACE SAFETY PROGRAM CHECKUP

Continued

B. Facility and equipment maintenance	18. ❐ Operators are trained to recognize maintenance needs and to perform and order maintenance on schedule. ❐ An effective preventive maintenance schedule is in place and applicable to all equipment. ❐ A preventive maintenance schedule is in place and is usually followed except for higher priorities.
	❐ A preventive maintenance schedule is in place but is often allowed to slide. ❐ There is little or no attention paid to preventive maintenance; breakdown maintenance is the rule.
C-1. Emergency planning and preparation	19. ❐ There is an effective emergency response plan, and employees know immediately how to respond as a result of effective planning, training, and drills. ❐ There is an effective emergency response plan, and employees have a good understanding of responsibilities as a result of plans, training, and drills.
	❐ There is an effective emergency response plan and team, but other employees may be uncertain of their responsibilities. ❐ There is an effective emergency response plan, but training and drills are weak and roles may be unclear. ❐ Little effort is made to prepare for emergencies.
C-2. Emergency equipment	20. ❐ Facility is fully equipped for emergencies; all systems and equipment are in place and regularly tested; all personnel know how to use equipment and communicate during emergencies. ❐ Facility is well equipped for emergencies with appropriate emergency phones and directions; most personnel know how to use equipment and communicate during emergencies.
	❐ Emergency phones, directions, and equipment are in place, but only emergency teams know what to do. ❐ Emergency phones, directions, and equipment are in place, but employees show little awareness. ❐ There is little or no effort made to provide emergency equipment and information.
D-1. Medical program (health providers) — *when appropriate*	21. ❐ Occupational health providers have visited the site and are fully involved. ❐ Occupational health providers are involved in hazard assessment. ❐ Occupational health providers are consulted about significant health concerns in addition to incidents.

	❏ Occupational health providers are available but normally concentrate on employees who get hurt.
	❏ Occupational health assistance is rarely requested or provided.
D-2. Medical program (emergency care)	22. ❏ Personnel fully trained in emergency medicine are always available on-site. ❏ Personnel with basic first-aid skills are always available on-site, all shifts. ❏ Either on-site or nearby community aid is always available on day shift. ❏ Personnel with basic first-aid skills are usually available, with community assistance nearby.
	❏ Neither on-site nor community aid can be ensured at all times.

IV. Workplace Safety Training

A. Employees learn hazards (how to protect themselves and others)	23. ❏ Facility is committed to high-quality employee hazard training, ensures that all participate, and provides regular updates; in addition, employees can demonstrate proficiency in, and support of, all areas covered by training. ❏ Facility is committed to high-quality employee hazard training, ensures all participate, and provides regular updates. ❏ Facility provides legally required training and makes an effort to include all employees.
	❏ Training is provided when the need is apparent; experienced employees are assumed to know the material. ❏ Facility depends on experience and informal peer training to meet needs.
B-1. Supervisors learn responsibilities and underlying reasons	24. ❏ All supervisors assist in work-site hazard analysis, ensure physical protections, reinforce training, enforce discipline, and can explain work procedures based on the training provided to them. ❏ Most supervisors assist in work-site hazard analysis, ensure physical protections, reinforce training, enforce discipline, and can explain work procedures based on the training provided to them. ❏ Supervisors have received basic training, appear to understand and demonstrate importance of work-site hazard analysis, physical protections, training reinforcement, discipline and knowledge of work procedures
	❏ Supervisors make an effort to meet workplace safety responsibilities but have limited training. ❏ There is no formal effort to train supervisors in workplace safety responsibilities.

WORKPLACE SAFETY PROGRAM CHECKUP

Continued

B-2. Managers learn workplace safety program management	25. ❏ All managers have received formal training in workplace safety management responsibilities. ❏ All managers follow, and can explain, their roles in workplace safety program management. ❏ Managers generally show a good understanding of their workplace safety roles and usually model them.
	❏ Managers are generally able to describe their workplace safety roles but often have trouble modeling them. ❏ Managers generally show little understanding of their workplace safety management responsibilities.

SAFETY AND HEALTH PROGRAM FOR SMALL BUSINESS EXAMPLE

This sample program follows the Occupational Safety and Health Administration's (OSHA) "Safety and Health Program Management Guidelines" (courtesy of OSHA). These guidelines were drawn from the experience obtained enforcing the OSHA Act, from the Voluntary Protection Programs (VPP), OSHA programs to recognize excellence in work-site safety and health, from OSHA's Consultation Program, and from public commentary. This sample program is especially written for the small independent business owner, but the outline can be applied to any size business.

Worksite Safety and Health Program

Management Leadership and Employee Involvement

Management commits the necessary resources of staff, money, and time to ensure that all persons on the work site are protected from injury and illness hazards. In addition, management visibly leads in the design, implementation, and continuous improvement of the site's safety and health activities. Specifically, the highest-level management establishes and reviews annually the site's safety and health policy and ensures that all employees know, understand, and support that policy. All management levels, with input from hourly employees, develop an annual safety and health goal with objectives and action plans to reach that goal. At the end of each year all management levels, with input from hourly employees, evaluate progress in accomplishing the action plans, achieving all objectives, and meeting the annual goal. This evaluation, which also includes an evaluation of the overall safety and health program, results in a written report that includes the next year's goal, objectives, and action plans, including any remaining action needed to accomplish the current year's goal.

Management ensures that all employees, including managers themselves, have clearly written safety and health responsibilities included within their job description, with appropriate authority to carry out those responsibilities. Also, management ensures that all employees, including all levels of management, receive performance evaluations that include a written evaluation of the accomplishment of assigned safety and health responsibilities.

Continued

Management ensures that all visitors to the site, including contract and temporary labor, co-op students, interns, vendors, and salespeople, have knowledge of site hazards applicable to them and how to protect themselves against those hazards, including emergency alarms and procedures. Management also ensures that these visitors do not introduce to the site hazards that can be prevented or that are not properly controlled.

Management ensures that at least several avenues exist for employee involvement in safety and health decision making and problem solving. These avenues may include serving on committees and ad hoc problem-solving groups, acting as safety observers, assisting in training other employees, analyzing hazards inherent in site jobs and how to protect against those hazards (writing JHAs), and planning activities to heighten safety and health awareness. Management encourages employees' involvement and devises appropriate recognition for outstanding employee participation.

Suggested Documents to Implement this Element

- Work-site policy (note how this policy is communicated to the work force and visitors)
- Current year's goals, objectives, action plans, and program evaluation
- Job descriptions that include safety and health responsibilities
- Performance evaluations that include an evaluation of safety and health responsibilities
- Budget showing money allocated to safety and health
- Contractor bidding proposal sheets showing all contractors' prior safety and health record
- Orientation outline for all site visitors, including contractors
- Evidence of employee involvement, such as committee minutes or other records of employee participation in safety and health program decisions

Work-Site Analysis

Management hires outside consultants as necessary to conduct baseline surveys that identify all safety and health hazards at the site at the time of the survey. All hazards found during these surveys are eliminated whenever possible or controlled. All employees who may encounter the controlled hazards are trained in appropriate job procedures to follow to protect themselves from these hazards.

Management establishes change procedures to follow whenever the site experiences changes in equipment, material, or processes. To ensure employee protection, these change procedures include consideration of safety and health in the selection of the change, equipment and process shutdown procedures, start-up procedures, and phase hazard analysis. Appropriate employees are trained to follow these procedures.

Management and employees work together to analyze safety and health hazards inherent in each job site and to find means to eliminate those hazards, whenever possible, and otherwise to protect persons against those hazards. These job hazard analyses (JHAs) are revised as appropriate (e.g., following a change in the job, the reappearance of a hazard, or an accident at this job).

All employees at this site are trained to recognize hazards and to report any hazard they find to the appropriate person so that the hazard can be corrected as soon as possible. In addition to taking immediate action to report a hazard orally and to provide interim protection, if necessary, including stopping the work causing the hazard, employees may submit a safety work order to the maintenance department or they may submit a safety suggestion form. Safety work orders take priority over any other work order. Safety suggestions will be considered each week during the site inspection by the site inspection team. All employee reports of hazards must be eventually written, with the correction date recorded. These reports are posted in the lunchroom until the hazard is corrected and then are kept on file in the owner's office for three years. During that time they are available for employee review.

Site management, with input from an hourly employee chosen by lot, organizes the monthly site inspection team. Membership on these teams rotates each month with the goal that all site employees serve one month each year. Teams consist of four people, two managers or supervisors, and two hourly employees. Each week, at the beginning of work on Wednesday morning, the team inspects the entire work site, describing in writing all hazards found, including their location. The team assigns appropriate persons responsible for seeing that the hazard is corrected and documenting the date of the correction. These inspection reports are posted in the lunchroom, in

Continued

the maintenance shop, and in the owner's office. A hazard remains on the monthly report until it is corrected.

Any near miss, first-aid incident, or accident is investigated by the trained team selected each year by the owner and an hourly employee. The team consists of two managers or supervisors and two hourly employees, each of whom has received training in accident investigation. All investigations have as a goal the identification of the root cause of the accident rather than assigning blame. All accident reports are posted in the lunchroom and are open to comment by any employee. The accident investigation team assigns responsibility to appropriate employees for correcting any hazards found and for assigning a date by which the correction must be completed.

As part of the annual safety and health program evaluation, the site owner, a manager, and an hourly employee review all near misses, first-aid incidents, and entries on the OSHA 300 Log, as well as employee reports of hazards, to determine if any pattern exists that can be addressed. The results of this analysis are considered in setting the goal, objectives, and action plans for the next year.

Suggested Documents to Implement This Element

- Results of baseline safety and health surveys, with notation of hazard correction
- Forms used for change analyses, including safety and health considerations in the purchase of new equipment, chemicals, or materials
- JHAs
- Employee reports of hazards
- Site safety and health inspection results, with hazard corrections noted
- Accident investigation reports, with hazard corrections noted
- Trend analyses results

Hazard Prevention and Control

Management ensures that the this priority is followed to protect persons at this site: (1) Hazards will be eliminated when economically feasible, such as replacing a more hazardous chemical with a less hazardous one; (2) Barriers will protect persons from the hazard, such as machine guards and personal protective equipment (PPE); (3) Exposure to hazards will be controlled through administrative procedures, such as more frequent breaks and job rotation.

Management ensures that the work site and all machinery is cared for properly so that the environment remains safe and healthy. If maintenance needs exceed the capability of the work-site employees, contract employees are hired to do the work and are screened and supervised to ensure they work according to the site's safety and health procedures.

All employees, including all levels of management, are held accountable for obeying site safety and health rules. This four-step disciplinary policy will be applied to everyone by the appropriate level of supervisor:

1. Oral warning
2. Written reprimand
3. Three days away from work
4. Dismissal

Visitors, including contractors who violate safety and health rules and procedures, will be escorted from the site. Should the disciplined person request a review of the disciplinary action, an ad hoc committee of six people, three managers and three hourly workers, chosen by their respective colleagues will review the situation and make a recommendation to the owner, who reserves the right for final decision. If his decision differs from that of the committee, he may, within confidentially strictures, make public his reasons.

Site management works with appropriate outside agencies, such as the fire department, the police department, and the hospital, to write emergency plans for all potential emergencies, including fire, explosion, accident, severe weather, loss of power and/or water, and violence from an outside source. Tabletop drills are conducted monthly so that all employees experience a drill on each type of emergency once a year. A total site evacuation drill focusing on one emergency type, with all work shut down, and coordinated with the appropriate agency, is conducted once a year. Each drill, whether tabletop or actual evacuation, is evaluated by the drill planning committee, constituted each year with two managers or supervisors and two hourly employees who volunteer. This committee's written report is posted in the lunchroom, and supervisors ensure that all employees know the results. When necessary, the emergency procedures are revised as a result of the evaluation report.

SAFETY AND HEALTH PROGRAM FOR SMALL
BUSINESS EXAMPLE

Continued

Persons needing emergency care are transported by company van
or community ambulance to the hospital, located five miles from the
site. Usually that trip can be made in less than 10 minutes. On-site
during all shifts designated persons fully trained in cardiac
pulmonary resuscitation (CPR), first aid, and the requirements of
OSHA's Bloodborne Pathogen Standard are the first responders to
any emergency. These persons are trained by qualified Red Cross
instructors. One of these designated persons' safety and health
responsibilities is to ensure that first-aid kits are stocked and readily
accessible in the marked locations throughout the plant. Appropriate
personal protective equipment (PPE) is provided for the different
types of accidents possible at the site. All emergency responders
have been offered the Hepatitis B vaccine.

Management maintains a proactive occupational health program
that provides for occupational health professionals from the local
hospital to participate in work-site analyses to find and protect
employees against all health hazards. This plan provides initial health
screening for each employee, appropriate to the hazards with which
each employee will be working, and for tracking of any health
changes in each employee through periodic physical examinations,
postexposure exams, and an exit exam. Certified industrial hygienists
conduct periodic air and noise monitoring.

The doctor and occupational health nurse, working on contract for
the site, examine health surveillance data to discern changes in
overall employee health screening results to discover any trends that
need to be addressed. Health professionals, appropriately trained
and knowledgeable about site hazards, immediately treat employees
for occupational health problems and follow each case until the
individual can return full-time to all aspects of his assigned job.
These professionals ensure that employee medical records are kept
confidentially so that diagnosis and treatment are not divulged, but
management does have information about the employee under
treatment as to:

- Ability to perform job tasks
- Job limitations or accommodations needed
- Length of time the limitations must be implemented

Management ensures that supervisors honor these restrictions. This healthcare is provided free of charge for all employees. The total plan is reviewed annually to assess its effectiveness.

Through consultants, management has assessed all work at this site and determined that the following OSHA standards apply to the site's work. Individual safety and health programs for each of these standards have been written and implemented. Employees affected by these standards have been trained to understand them and to follow the programs' directions. These standards are:

Hazard Communication
Hearing Conservation
Bloodborne Pathogens Program
Confined Space Program
Lockout/Tagout
Emergency Evacuation Program
Required PPE, Including Respiratory Protection

Suggested Documents to Implement This Element

- Preventive maintenance schedule
- Disciplinary program and records
- Site rules
- Written programs mandated by OSHA
- Maintenance records
- Emergency drill procedures and critiques
- Health surveillance and monitoring records
- Reports and investigations of near misses, first aid, and OSHA 300 logs

Training

Management believes that employee involvement in the site's safety and health program can be successful only when everyone on the site receives sufficient training to understand what their safety and health responsibilities and opportunities are and how to fulfill them. Therefore, training is a high priority to ensure a safe and healthy workplace. Finding time and knowledgeable personnel to do effective training is vital. Each year management pays special attention to the evaluation of the year's training efforts to look for methods of improvement.

Currently all new employees receive two hours of safety and health orientation before they begin work. When they have learned

Continued

this material, they begin their assigned job with a trained buddy. For
the first day, the employee only observes the buddy doing the job
and reads the appropriate JHAs. The second day, the new employee
does the job, while the buddy observes him/her. For the first six
months on the job a new employee is considered a probationer and
may not work beyond the line of vision of another employee.
Supervisors are strictly charged to ensure that this training process is
followed for all new employees and for any employee beginning a
new job at the work site.

All employees are paid for one full day's work (eight hours)
beyond their production schedule each pay period. This time is
usually split into several sections to attend training classes. A list of
training topics, by week, is published each year. Each topic is offered
at least twice. Each employee is responsible for ensuring that he/she
masters the year's training topics. Completing the year's training is a
significant portion of the performance evaluation for all employees,
including all levels of management. Training records are kept by the
personnel manager and are available for employee review, upon
request.

All employees are encouraged to suggest qualified trainers,
including themselves. Management is responsible for ensuring that
all training offered at the site is conducted by qualified persons.

Suggested Documents to Implement This Element

- List of yearly training topics with name of trainer and his/her
  qualifications
- Yearly training class schedule with attendance lists
- Individual employee training records with evidence of subject
  mastery

MANAGER/SUPERVISOR INCIDENT INVESTIGATION REPORT EXAMPLE

The purpose of an investigation is to help prevent similar incidents from happening again.

1. Date of Report: _____ Incident Date: _____ Time: _____ AM/PM

2. Injured staff member's name: _____

3. Occupation: _____ Months on the job: _____

4. Where did the incident occur?

_____

_____

_____

5. Describe the injury.

_____

_____

_____

6. What was the employee doing when injured?

_____

_____

_____

_____

_____

7. What actions or conditions contributed to the incident?

_____

_____

_____

_____

_____

_____

MANAGER/SUPERVISOR INCIDENT INVESTIGATION REPORT EXAMPLE

Continued

8. **What do you recommend be done (or have you done) to prevent this type of incident from happening again?**

_____

_____

_____

_____

9. **Investigation done by:** _____ **Date:** _____

10. **Report reviewed by:** _____ **Date:** _____

Complete within <u>one day</u> of injury.

Guidelines for successfully completing this report

1. **Date and Time of incident.**
2. **Name of injured staff member.**
3. **Job title and number of months on the job of injured staff member.**
4. **Identify the location and the area in which the incident occurred. Example:** *In office area*
5. **Describe the injury. Example:** *Injury to right knee*
6. **Identify what the employee was doing when injured.**
   Example: *While moving a case, it fell over on employee's right knee.*
7. **Identify any unsafe acts or conditions that may have contributed to the cause of the incident.**
   Example of an unsafe act: *The case the employee was moving is very heavy. By asking for help, this injury may have been prevented.*
   Example of an unsafe condition: *While moving the case, employee's shoe caught in the torn carpet in the hallway. (Torn carpet could be an unsafe behavior if it had previously noted.)*
8. **Your recommendations. Example:** *To minimize the possibility of this happening again:*
   1. *Fix torn carpeting in hallway (use duct tape as a temporary fix).*
   2. *Remind employee that she can ask for help when doing certain tasks.*
   3. *Have employee discuss the incident at our next staff meeting. She could give some recommendations to other employees on how to prevent a similar injury from occurring in the future.*
9. **Investigations *are best conducted by someone with basic incident investigation training.***
10. **Report is reviewed by the safety committee (or other designated group).**

SECURITY MANAGEMENT PLAN EXAMPLE

Element 1: Policy Statement

(Security Management is an important enough topic that developing a policy statement, and publishing it with the program, is a critical consideration. The policy statement can be extracted and included in a new-hire employment packet and employee handbook, or placed on the company's intranet site.)

A policy statement might read in part:

> We are committed to maintaining the security and well-being of our employees, visitors, and the surrounding community. Our security management program is but one aspect of our overall workplace safety efforts. Together, these efforts span personnel, information, and asset security and include training and education activities to help ensure our programs' success. Additionally we will diligently work to comply with all applicable laws, regulations, and standards.
>
> Responsibility for this program has been vested with each department manager. Your cooperation with their efforts will help us all maintain a program that accomplishes all of its goals.
>
> We take specific actions toward identifying security-related threats, including workplace violence, and threats that may exist from domestic or foreign terrorism. You (employees) can expand these efforts by reporting concerns and any security breaches immediately.
>
> Your ongoing knowledge and cooperation as well as participation with the security program's efforts will be appreciated and help ensure its success.

Element 2: Compliance with Applicable Laws, Regulations, and Standards

(Comment: To the extent that laws and regulations exist, the plan should delineate efforts to comply and how you will comply. All of the compliance efforts may not need to be repeated within an employee handbook, for example, but should be tactical elements of a program. Some jurisdictions have not mandated specific plans, but have elements of applicable OSHA regulations, such as the General Duty Clause. In that case, indicate those that do apply. In this example, we'll use a California-based company.)

Various laws, regulations, and standards apply to our program. We will comply with, at a minimum:

- Cal/OSHA General Duty Clause T8CCR Section 3203
- Cal/OSHA Emergency Action Plans T8CCR Section 3220
- Cal/OSHA's Guidelines regarding Workplace Security

Continued

As other laws or regulations are introduced, we will integrate their provisions into our program.

Element 3: Definitions

(Comment: In this section, define terms not readily understood by all. The inclusion of definitions will help those who have to read and deploy the program and assist in training efforts.)

- Access controls related to access to your facilities
- Bomb threats—threats received that a bomb may be detonated
- OSHA—Occupational Safety & Health Administration
- Emergency operations center—location where management team meets
- Incident reporting—steps necessary to capture information about a threat or incident
- Response protocols—steps to follow in an actual event
- Terrorism—domestic or foreign acts
- Threats—verbal, written, actual or perceived
- Training—training related to the Security Management Program
- Workplace violence—events within your establishment that threaten or result in harm
- Others: [fill-in]

Definitions critical to any Security Management Program will be included as they are learned.

Element 4: Management Commitment and Responsibilities

(Comments: Delineate, either in narrative or in outline form, the responsibilities of senior management, management, and supervision, if their responsibilities differ. These responsibilities can be preceded, if necessary, by an internal use management commitment statement.)

Management commitment and responsibilities include:
- Program management
- Program review and updates
- Development of a review panel or task force if hazards are identified, or for deployment after an event to assist in its review
- Assisting with training

- Enforcing disciplinary actions as needed
- Interaction and assistance with regulatory and response agencies

This section can also include responsibilities for employees, especially those occupying specific roles (by position, not name).

Element 5: Threat Assessment and Analysis

(Comment: A core element of a security management program is the identification of internal and external threats. Delineate the mechanisms for identifying threats in this section, detailing when assessments will be conducted, who will conduct assessments, and how findings will be modified at future dates if need be.)

Security threat assessments will be:

- Completed prior to the initiation of this program
- Will be conducted as we become aware of new or potential threats
- Conducted for special events that we are either sponsoring or attending

Our security management committee under the direction of the [general manager] will conduct threat assessments on a scheduled or as required basis. The use of other internal or external resources might be necessary as well.

Threats will be qualified utilizing a threat matrix or other tool that compares operations to threats and their likelihood and severity. Where possible, mitigating actions and recommendations will be initiated. The threat matrix, after its initial completion and after any updates or modification, will be submitted to senior management for review and approval.

Element 6: The Role of the Security Program Manager

(Comments: Remember, even though the term *security* is being used, and this program should be integrated with overall workplace safety activities, an organization may have an existing security department. Alternate terminology may be needed if the two programs remain distinct and report to different managers.)

The role of the security manager includes:

- Lead role in threat assessments
- Program maintenance and updates

SECURITY MANAGEMENT PLAN EXAMPLE

Continued

- Incident response and coordination
- Chair of the security program committee
- Training responsibilities
- Coordination with other departments
- Coordination with agencies and response units

Element 7: Employee Education and Training
(Comments: Distinguish general awareness/educational from the tactical duties or training activities that are required.)

Our program will cover:

- Employee duties and responsibilities
- Event-specific responsibilities
- Threat or event reporting
- Back-to-work/check-in requirements
- Potential disciplinary actions
- Dealing with the media, regulatory agencies, or other entities outside the company

Element 8: Management and Supervisor Education and Training
(Comments: Managers and supervisors likely will have specific duties and expectations, ranging from threat identification and mitigation to their role in event response. Some of the responsibilities may mirror those of the employees but are likely more specific in event-response scenarios.)

For managers and supervisors, our program focuses on:

- Individual or department duties
- Knowledge and deployment of response protocols
- Ensuring employee and other constituent welfare
- Threat or event reporting
- Back-to-work/check-in requirements
- Potential disciplinary actions
- Dealing with the media, regulatory agencies, or other entities outside the company

Element 9: Program Exercises and Drills
(Comments: The training and education activities undertaken for the purposes of the security management program shall be: case studies, tabletop exercises, or small- and/or large-scale exercises.

The appropriate methodology for training and education shall be at the discretion of the program manager.

Case Studies

Case studies are in essence, paper-and-pen exercises. They provide an excellent opportunity to educate employees about the program, their responsibilities, and basic response protocols. It is assumed that most case studies are conducted in a classroom setting, but in some instances, "homework" may be appropriate. In such cases, it is essential to have follow-up discussions to determine that the case study participant clearly understood what was being discussed in the assigned materials.

The goal of case studies is to ensure knowledge of plans, procedures, and job functions related to threat management, response, and event-dependent administrative activities that may be assigned.

Other case study dynamics include:

- They must represent real-world scenarios.
- They are ideally suited for initial program education as well as that which is specific to a department or specific scenario.

Case studies will be the primary educational activity for most employees. Where necessary or required, training sessions will be provided as well. Case study sessions will, at a minimum, include the procedures to follow in the event of:

- Bomb threat
- Violence-in-the-workplace situation, potential or actual
- Domestic violence occurring within our facilities
- General evacuation requirements due to a technical, human or natural threat
- Others as may be determined by the general manager or security management committee, as examples

Case studies will be a required element of initial training for new employees and will occur on an annual basis for all employees at a minimum. All employees will participate in case studies.

Tabletop Exercises

Tabletop exercises expand the scenarios and number of participants to include multiple departments. However, tabletop exercises may be conducted to test only one department's capabilities.

Tabletop exercises are more rigorous and complex than case studies. They also are sound vehicles to ascertain that threat management and response duties are understood and can be implemented.

SECURITY MANAGEMENT PLAN EXAMPLE

Continued

The goals of tabletop exercises are to validate response and event management capabilities and to test specific protocols under simulated event conditions.

Review sessions will be conducted at the conclusion of tabletop exercises, chaired by the security manager. Such sessions shall review the successes of the exercise, areas requiring improvement, and necessary program modifications.

The results of the exercise shall be summarized and submitted to the management team.

Tabletop exercises will be used for several purposes, primarily as expanded education and training tools for supervisors and those who are responsible to help manage an event or are responsible for event communications. In addition to the scenarios highlighted in case studies, others that will be included in tabletop exercises at a minimum will include:

- Large-scale natural event, such as an earthquake
- Employee assault with a weapon
- Terrorism, including bioterrorism

Tabletop exercises will be conducted quarterly at the direction of the general manager. Supervisors and Lead personnel will participate in tabletop exercises.

Small-Scale Drills

Small-scale drills may also be referred to as functional drills. They are intended to test the interaction of multiple departments and may involve outside agencies or mutual aid partners.

Activation of the emergency operations center (EOC) is recommended during small-scale exercises. Small-scale exercises are designed to test and validate established response plans and capabilities. In addition, such exercises test the availability of resources and materials in the time of need, including, for example, communications equipment and first-aid supplies.

Small-scale drills are scenario-based as opposed to general in nature. Thus, based on need, multiple drills may be conducted in any given time period or may be instituted to test a new procedure or response protocols.

Subsequent to small-scale drills, a review session will be conducted to analyze response dynamics, drill success, and areas that need improvement. Findings and documentation of the drill will be provided to the security program management committee.

Small-scale exercises may require the participation of some supervisors and will require the participation of most management personnel, due to their more aggressive nature and decision-making elements. In addition to the scenarios outlined in the case studies and tabletop exercises, these potential events, at a minimum, will be included in small-scale exercise planning and activities:

- Regional natural event, such as an earthquake
- Intruder with weapon
- Bioterrorism event
- Political activist
- Regional or facility-specific power failure

Small-scale exercises will be held as required or as situations mandate; however, our plan calls for two small-scale exercises per year at a minimum. Supervisors and Managers will participate in small-scale exercises.

Large-Scale Drills

Large-scale drills are designed to test the entire capability of the security management program. This includes reporting, event communications, managing events, utilization of the EOC, interaction with outside agencies and mutual aid partners, as well as ensuring that vendors and suppliers can meet their responsibilities at the time of an event.

(Note: At no time should *any* exercises be conducted that place at risk the health and safety of personnel, the community at large, and guests/visitors to operations. Safety must be considered at all times during the planning and conduct of such activities.)

Large-scale exercises are more complex to produce, as they require considerable planning and resource requirements. Wherever possible (and safe), actual operational disruption to simulate an event should be made part of the exercise.

In large-scale exercises, the EOC or similar management location and structure shall be activated.

Large-scale exercises, at a minimum, shall test these program elements:

- Event recognition
- Communications—equipment and messages
- Employee, supervisory, and management response
- Compliance with established protocols

Continued

- Utilization of security management plans
- Utilization of resources established to assist us to recognize, respond, and recover from an event
- Utilization of other resources
- Communication with mutual aid partners
- Activation and utilization of the EOC
- Communication and coordination with essential vendors and suppliers

During the course of large-scale exercises, it is recommended that:

- Observers from selected sources be involved as outside exercise reviewers.
- Multiple scenario planning is implemented. That is, the exercise should recognize the dynamic nature of emergency events and that rarely, if ever, is a single event resolved without other subevents occurring that also require management.

Large-scale exercises shall be conducted no less often than annually.

Findings of the exercise shall be summarized and submitted to the management team for review and comment.

Large-scale exercises may include any of the threats noted in the case studies, tabletop and/or small-scale discussions. Large-scale exercises will include employees, lead and supervisory personnel, management, and senior management representatives. Scenario planning will be the responsibility of the general manager and security manager.

It is our intent to hold one large-scale exercise per year at a minimum. More may be required due to event development or specific hazard concerns, such as adverse weather patterns or terrorist threats.

Element 10: Specific Program Considerations

Our security management program includes specific considerations for:

- Identification systems
- Facility access
- Access controls

(Comments: Insert into this section your company's requirements for identifying personnel, vendors, and guests. This section will also include requirements for facility access and the controls that have been implemented. Do not include any codes, passwords, or other descriptors that could be used to compromise security-related systems.)

Element 11: Threat Mitigation, Control and Response

(Comments: As threats are identified, every effort shall be made to eliminate, mitigate, or control them.)

This section of our program describes responsibilities for:

- Mitigating and controlling threats
- Specific responsibilities
- Confirming and documenting control efforts
- The Human Resources Department role in threat mitigation, especially regarding threats emanating from or directed toward personnel

Threat response, other than that which has been delineated specifically, includes:

- Safety first. Our goal is to assume the safety of employees as well as all of our constituents. Any actions taken to respond to a threat must be taken with safety as our first goal. If questions arise regarding safety and health, they must immediately be directed to the security program manager.

Element 12: Incident Review and Analysis

(Comments: All incidents and responses will be viewed by the management team and other internal representatives where necessary.)

This section describes our:

- Forms to be utilized during the review process
- Process for review and analysis
- Requirements for documentation
- Process to ensure program updates and enhancements are appropriately integrated

Element 13: Specific Response Protocols

(Comment: You will have to decide what specific threats may need their own protocols within your company.)

Where general response protocols will not suffice for particular threats, these specific response protocols apply:

- Bomb threats
- Terrorism
- Workplace violence

Continued

Element 14: Mutual Aid

(Comment: Where mutual aid agreements are critical to the success of your program, they should be made part of your plan. Include how to get in touch with all of the mutual aid partners and what their specific role and/or obligations are.)

Our mutual aid agreements extend to:

- Business partners
- Possibly municipal relationships
- Contractually obligated organizations
- Recovery partners

Element 15: Communications

(Comments: This section should list communication tactics, options, equipment, and so on, including those that may be included in the emergency operations center.)

Element 16: Programs Included by Reference

(Comments: Include in this section other programs that you feel need to be incorporated. The best example might be your workplace safety program or certain aspects of it, where specific safety and health measures may apply for those responsible for responding to events. Your emergency response program should be incorporated as well.)

Element 17: Appendices

These items are included as critical elements within the security management program:

- Training outlines and documentation
- Call-out lists: numbers and alternates
- Mutual aid agreements
- Maps
- Blueprints, floor plans, evacuation maps
- Area map
- Government agency (FBI, Police, Fire, etc.) contact information

ACTIVITY CALENDAR EXAMPLE

The Activity Calendar identifies major activities and milestones to be accomplished each year for your workplace safety program. From time to time, these milestones will change, especially regarding training topics, which may change based on operations, regulatory mandate, or changes in actual hazards and/or personnel.

The calendar is comprehensive. It is essential that, for each activity, applicable delegation of responsibility for completion take place. Once any activity is completed, it should be appropriately documented.

Workplace Safety Master Calendar

January
- ☐ Annual Program Audit
- ☐ General Codes of Safe Practice—Review and Distribute
- ☐ Annual Workplace Safety Reiteration Memo
- ☐ Complete and Prepare OSHA 300 for Posting
- ☐ Annual Update on Safety to "All Staff"
- ☐ Safety Committee Meeting
- ☐ Medical Monitoring and Fit-Testing (as needed)
- ☐ Shop Talk (= Department Training)
- ☐ Training: Lock-Out/Tag-Out
- ☐ Tailgate: Field Operations*
- ☐ Annual Poster/Posting Notice Assessment

February
- ☐ Report on Annual Program Audit
- ☐ Comprehensive Plant Inspection
- ☐ Post OSHA Log Summary (by February 1)
- ☐ Review Unit Status Report
- ☐ Management Training
- ☐ Medical Monitoring and Fit-Testing (as needed)
- ☐ Shop Talk
- ☐ Training: Fire Prevention and Emergency Action Plans
- ☐ Tailgate: Field Operations*

March
- ☐ Check Department of Motor Vehicles (DMV) Records of Drivers
- ☐ WC Claims Review Meeting
- ☐ First Aid Supply Review
- ☐ First Aid Training (if selected)
- ☐ Fleet Inspection
- ☐ Medical Monitoring and Fit-Testing (as needed)
- ☐ Shop Talk
- ☐ Training: Ergonomics
- ☐ Tailgate: Field Operations*

Continued

April
- ☐ Safety Committee Meeting
- ☐ Management Training
- ☐ Review and Update PPE Matrix
- ☐ Chemical Inventory/Update Material Safety Data Sheets (MSDS)
- ☐ Remove OSHA Log Summary (no sooner than April 30)
- ☐ Medical Monitoring and Fit-Testing (as needed)
- ☐ Shop Talk
- ☐ Training: Fall Protection
- ☐ Tailgate: Field Operations*

May
- ☐ Specific Codes of Safe Practice Review and Update
- ☐ Management Training Update Important Phone Numbers
- ☐ Medical Monitoring and Fit-Testing (as needed)
- ☐ Shop Talk
- ☐ Training: Forklift Operations
- ☐ Tailgate: Field Operations*

June
- ☐ Driver "Ride-Alongs"
- ☐ Specific Codes of Safe Practice Review and Update
- ☐ Fleet Inspection
- ☐ Overall Recordkeeping Review
- ☐ Management Injury and Illness Review (WC and OSHA 300)
- ☐ Medical Monitoring and Fit-Testing (as needed)
- ☐ Shop Talk
- ☐ Training: Fleet and Driver Safety
- ☐ Tailgate: Field Operations*

July
- ☐ Update Hazard Management Activities/Document
- ☐ Safety Committee Meeting
- ☐ Medical Monitoring and Fit-Testing (as needed)
- ☐ Preparation for WC Renewal
- ☐ WC Claims Review Meeting
- ☐ Shop Talk
- ☐ Training: Confined Spaces and Respiratory Protection
- ☐ Tailgate: Field Operations*

August
- ☐ Training Matrix Review and Update
- ☐ Training Calendar Review and Update

- ❐ Review and Update Forms Catalog
- ❐ Medical Monitoring and Fit-Testing (as needed)
- ❐ Shop Talk
- ❐ Training: Hazard Communication
- ❐ Tailgate: Field Operations*

September
- ❐ Management Training
- ❐ Fleet Inspection
- ❐ WC Claims Review Meeting
- ❐ Medical Monitoring and Fit-Testing (as needed)
- ❐ Shop Talk
- ❐ Training: Office Ergonomics/Safety
- ❐ Tailgate: Field Operations*

October
- ❐ Safety Committee Meeting
- ❐ Chemical Inventory/Update MSDSs
- ❐ Medical Monitoring and Fit-Testing (as needed)
- ❐ Shop Talk
- ❐ Management Activity: Incident Investigation Training
- ❐ Training: Hearing Conservation
- ❐ Tailgate: Field Operations*

November
- ❐ Review Field Workplace Safety Manual and republish (as necessary)
- ❐ Forms Review and Update
- ❐ Medical Monitoring and Fit-Testing (as needed)
- ❐ Shop Talk
- ❐ Training: Workplace Security**
- ❐ Tailgate: Field Operations*

December
- ❐ Driver "Ride-alongs"
- ❐ Safety Committee Meeting
- ❐ Overall Recordkeeping Review
- ❐ Medical Monitoring and Fit-Testing (as needed)
- ❐ Shop Talk
- ❐ Training: Confined Spaces
- ❐ Tailgate: Field Operations*

* May be required more frequently.
** Optional

PROGRAM AUDIT—SUMMARY RATING

Organization: _____

Department/Function: _____ **Date:** _____ **Completed by:** _____

Category	[0–1+] Poor	[2–5+] Fair	[6–8+] Good	[9–10] Excl.	N/A	Total	Comments on Rating
1. IIPP							
2. Standard Operating Procedures or Risks (JHAs)							
3. Safety Responsibilities							
4. Group Safety Talks							
5. Inspections							
6. Training							
7. Accident Reporting and Investigation							
8. Housekeeping							
9. Emergency Procedures							
10. Safety Committees							
11. Equipment/Tool Use and Maintenance							
12. Personal Protective Equipment							
13. Material Handling							
14. Chemical Safety/ Hazard Communication							
15. Noise Control							
16. Fleet Operations							

Continued

PROGRAM AUDIT—SUMMARY RATING

Continued

Other. Note: No points assessed for A–F; they are used as differentiators in #1–16.

A. Employee Orientation							
B. Employee Placement							
C. Return to Work for Injured Employees							
D. Supervisor Safety Responsibilities							
E. Employee Safety Responsibilities							
F. First Aid							

Total Points: _____   Previous Points: _____

Discussion: _____

_____

_____

_____

_____

Instructions: Include the appropriate numbers within the rating category boxes. Total the rows and columns (these totals should match) and enter the total on the bottom of the page. Compare these results to previous or future audits. Note: Develop the rating criteria for each of the categories—Poor, Fair, Good or Excellent.

oing training and professional
lopment for industrial hygienists,
 of whom have received
alized certification to practice in
eld.

**an Medical Association
A)** A national physician's group.
AMA publishes a set of guidelines
 "Guides to the Evaluation of
nent Impairment." If your
nent disability is rated under the
ating schedule, the doctor is
d to determine your level of
ment using the AMA's guides.

**n National Standards
te (ANSI)** A voluntary
rship organization (run with
funding) that develops
us standards nationally for a
riety of devices and
res.

**s with Disabilities Act
** A federal law that prohibits
ation against people with
s.

**Society of Industrial
(ASIS)** An educational
ntialing society focused on
fessionals who practice
security, including assets,
, and processes. The ASIS
e professional designation
ified Protection
al).

**ociety of Safety Engineers
** he nation's oldest
al health and safety
 in the United States,
 practicing safety
 and associate members.
 provides ongoing
opportunities and essential
 on regulatory matters and
 to the dozens of local
ss the country.

**Annual Survey of Occupational
Injuries and Illnesses (ASOII)** A
survey conducted annually by the
Bureau of Labor Statistics on a
national level. Some employers are
required to participate, while others
do so voluntarily. This survey is a
large-scale summary of the
information found on OSHA logs and
other relevant injury and illness data.

ANSI *See* American National Standards
Institute.

AOE/COE A term utilized within the
workers' compensation field, the
acronym for *arising out of and occurring
in the course of employment*. For claims
(work injury cases) to be accepted for
compensability or disability, they must
have occurred AOE/COE.

Apportionment In some states, a way
of figuring out how much permanent
disability is due.

ARM Associate in Risk Management.
This is a professional designation
offered by the Insurance Institute of
America in Malvern, Pennsylvania.
The ARM is earned after passing a
series of national examinations.

ASIS *See* American Society of Industrial
Security.

ASOII *See* Annual Survey of
Occupational Injuries and Illnesses.

ASSE *See* American Society of Safety
Engineers.

Biohazard A combination of the words
biological hazard. It is used to refer to
organisms or products of organisms
that present a risk to humans.

Biological safety A specialized area
within the field of occupational safety
and health. Biological safety or
"biosafety" has as its goal the
protection of workers from hazards

Glossary

Accident A sudden, unexplained event; often used for those events that result in injuries or illness.

ACGIH *See* American Conference of Governmental Industrial Hygienists.

ACOEM *See* American College of Occupational and Environmental Medicine.

Acute Happening quickly, usually associated with injuries; as opposed to chronic.

ADA *See* Americans with Disabilities Act.

Adjuster A person who investigates and settles insurance claims.

Agent A person who sells insurance policies.

AIHA *See* American Industrial Hygiene Association.

Air The mixture of gases that surrounds the earth; its major components are: 78.08% nitrogen, 20.95% oxygen, 0.03% carbon dioxide, and 0.93% argon. Water vapor (humidity) varies.

Alternative work A new job with your former employer. If your doctor says you will not be able to return to your job at the time of injury, your employer is encouraged to offer you alternative work instead of supplemental job displacement benefits

or voca
The al
work r
month
and b
you v
reaso
whei

AMA
Ass

Amer
an
(A
th
o
p
o
Α
(

An

Α

ong
dev
mos
spec
the

Ameri
(AM
The
called
Perm
perm
2005
requir
impai

America
Institu
memb
private
consen
wide v
procedu

American
(ADA)
discrimi
disabiliti

American
Security
and cred
those pro
industrial
personne
oversees t
CPP (Cer
Profession

American S
(ASSE) T
occupation
organizatio
representin
professional
The society
educational
information
is the parent
chapters acro

created by the manipulation of biological life-forms. Containment, decontamination, and protective equipment procedures are used to reduce the hazards from agents of disease such as bacteria and viruses.

Bloodborne pathogens Disease-causing microorganisms present in human blood. These pathogens include, but are not limited to, hepatitis B virus (HBV), hepatitis C virus (HCV), and human immunodeficiency virus (HIV).

BLS *See* Bureau of Labor Statistics.

Bureau of Labor Statistics (BLS) One of the preeminent sources of injury and illness-related statistics. In addition, the BLS publishes annual surveys taken from employer injury and illness records. Such information is utilized by businesses and regulatory agencies to focus their control and program efforts.

Carpal tunnel (CTS) An anatomic tunnel in the wrist through which the median nerve and nine digital flexor tendons pass. It is formed by the wrist bones and a dense transcarpal ligament. Pressure on the median nerve in the carpal tunnel causes carpal tunnel syndrome.

CFR *See* Code of Federal Regulations.

Chemical Hygiene Plan Required by Federal Regulation 29 CFR 1910 (and various state plans). The plan establishes safety standards for workers exposed to hazardous chemicals in laboratories. A written plan to implement control measures, training, and other protective measures is required of laboratories meeting specified criteria.

Chronic Continual exposure, repeated exposure, as opposed to acute; usually associated with illnesses.

Chronic effect An adverse effect on a human or animal body, with symptoms that develop slowly over a long period of time or which recur frequently. *Also see* acute.

Claim form The form used to report a work injury or illness to your employer.

Claimant A person who makes an insurance claim.

Claims adjuster/administrator/ examiner The term for insurance companies and others that handle your workers' compensation claims. Most claims administrators work for insurance companies or third-party administrators handling claims for employers. Some work directly for large employers that handle their own claims.

Code of Federal Regulations (CFR) A collection of the regulations that have been promulgated under U.S. law.

Code of safe practices A set of workplace rules that stipulate how to perform job duties safely and to keep the worksite safe. It must be specific to the employer's operations and posted at each job site office or be readily available at the job site. Workers must be directed to read it when they are first hired.

Collective bargaining agreement An agreement negotiated between a labor union and an employer that details the terms of employment for the employees subject to the agreement. This agreement may include provisions governing wages, vacation time, working hours, working conditions, and health insurance benefits.

Commission(s) In the context of insurance, a percentage of an organization's insurance premium that is paid to an insurance agent or broker.

Confined spaces Spaces in workplaces in which their configurations hinder the activities of any employees who must enter, work in, and exit them.

Construction safety orders (CSO) Regulations found in federal and state OSHA regulations that are specific to construction operations and hazard controls.

Crisis A time of turmoil or events that brings specific focus and attention to an organization, impacting reputation and requiring specialized skills in communication, leadership. and decision making.

CSO *See* construction safety orders.

CT *See* cumulative injury.

CTS *See* carpal tunnel syndrome.

Cumulative injury (CT) An injury that was caused by repeated events or repeated exposures at work. Examples include a wrist injury caused by doing the same motion over and over or a loss of hearing because of constant loud noise.

Date of injury The specific date when someone became hurt or ill. When the injury is caused by one event, the date it happened is the date of injury. In most states, if injury or illness was caused by repeated exposures (a cumulative injury), the date of injury is the date of knowledge that the injury was caused by work.

Death benefits Benefits paid to surviving dependents when a work injury or illness results in death.

Denied claim In some states, an injury case in which the insurance company believes an injury or illness is not covered by workers' compensation.

Department of Labor (DOL) A cabinet-level department responsible for the agencies that oversee safety and health in the United States, such as the Occupational Safety and Health Administration (OSHA) and the Mine Safety and Health Administration.

Deposition A formal session in which an attorney asks questions of a party under oath. It is the equivalent of testifying at a trial. The testimony is recorded by a court reporter and may be used as evidence in a trial situation.

Disability *See* permanent disability.

Disaster An event that overwhelms the resources and capabilities of an organization (e.g., catastrophic).

Disaster Recovery Institute International (DRII) Oversees training, education, and professional development for professionals in the broad field of business continuity. The DRII also is responsible for establishing the testing criteria and administering the national tests

DOL *See* Department of Labor.

DRII *See* Disaster Recovery Institute International.

Dusts Various types of solid particles that are produced when organic or inorganic materials are crushed, abraded, ground, sawed, and so forth.

EAP *See* employee assistance program.

Early Suppression, Fast Response (ESFR) Examples include sprinkler and fire protection systems.

Education As used in this text, those activities that provide general awareness regarding safety issues and regulations; designed to provide information and background material to assist someone in understanding critical safety concerns.

Emergency disaster plan A plan prepared by organizations to provide a swift, efficient, and cost-effective response to medical, fire, care and shelter, and communications needs after disasters.

Emergency preparedness Planning and actions undertaken in advance of a possible or probable disaster. Preparation of an emergency disaster plan is one component of emergency preparedness, but construction design, food and sanitation equipment storage, and conducting drills are also included.

Employee A person whose work activities are under the control of an individual or entity. The term includes undocumented workers and minors.

Employee assistance programs (EAPs) Critical adjuncts to safety and health efforts. Employees who are under stress or exhibiting behaviors that may create an unsafe work environment can be referred to an EAP for assistance. EAPs are staffed by psychologists, psychiatrists, and other mental health professionals. An EAP may be a first line of defense and a referral source for employees who are exhibiting tendencies toward becoming violent in the workplace.

Employee exposure records Information, results, or records concerning employee exposures to toxic or harmful substances or agents in the workplace. Examples are work area sampling results, biological monitoring results (e.g., blood tests), inventories of chemicals, and material safety data sheets.

Employee medical records Records concerning the health status of employees that are made by physicians, nurses, or other health professionals.

Examples include results of medical examinations, first-aid records, medical complaints, and diagnoses, opinions, and treatments recommended by a physician.

Environmental Protection Agency (EPA) The national agency that oversees the U.S programs that focus on environmental protection, pollution, pollution remediation, and the state programs managing similar concerns. The EPA, for example, oversees Superfund sites—those sites that are extensively polluted and require cleanup.

EPA *See* Environmental Protection Agency.

Ergonomics (workplace definition) The study of how to improve the fit between the physical demands of the workplace and the employees who perform the work. That means considering the variability in human capabilities when selecting, designing, or modifying equipment, tools, work tasks, and the work environment.

ESFR *See* Early Suppression, Fast Response.

Etiology The cause or origin of disease or study of the causes of disease.

Experience period The period of time that a company will refer to when evaluating an insurance policy.

Exposure An epidemiological concept used to describe the particular risk factor experienced by the worker, with its particular profile of modifying factors: intensity, time characteristics, and duration.

Federal Register A daily publication of the U.S. Government that highlights recently promulgated laws, rules and regulations.

Fire and life safety program A plan implemented by businesses and other organizations to protect constituents (e.g., employees, building occupants, etc.) from fire and other hazards that are immediately hazardous to life. Used here, such a program entails such elements as fire prevention, pre-fire planning, assessment of building design for compliance with fire and safety codes, ensuring proper emergency egress, and avoidance of electrical hazards or oxygen-deficient atmospheres, among other things.

First aid Emergency measures to be taken before regular medical help can be obtained.

Fraud (workers' compensation) Any knowingly false or fraudulent statement for the purpose of obtaining or denying workers' compensation benefits.

Frequency A term commonly used by safety professionals as a measure of how often injuries and illnesses occur and can be expressed as a raw number or in some form of a rate or ratio.

Fumes Solid particles that develop after having been volatilized while being heated; arise from metals and plastics for the most part.

Gases Formless fluids that may be toxic; one of the forms a hazardous substance can take.

General Industry Safety Orders (GISO) Federal or state OSHA orders that apply to all businesses across the board.

GISO *See* General Industry Safety Orders.

Hazard A condition with the potential to cause harm or physical damage

Hazard control program A formal written program that has been prepared and implemented to control one or more types of occupational health and safety hazards, or to prevent degradation of the environment. These programs are usually prepared to provide protection against specific types of hazards (e.g., ionizing radiation) or in response to regulatory requirements (e.g., a hazard awareness and communication program). Hazard control programs usually describe requirements and assign specific responsibilities for meeting those requirements. In many cases, hazard control programs list specific instructions that must be followed in managing certain hazards.

HCO *See* health care organization.

Health A condition of well-being, mental and physical.

Health care organization (HCO) In some states, an organization to provide managed medical care within the workers' compensation system.

Health hazards Substances that pose a health hazard through either acute (immediate) or chronic (long-term) toxicity. Examples of substances that are acutely toxic are sodium cyanide and ammonium molybdate; many organics, such as aniline derivatives, chlorinated hydrocarbons, and thiocyanates, cause chronic toxicity.

IARC *See* International Agency for Research on Cancer.

IDLH *See* immediately dangerous to life and health.

IIPP *See* injury and illness prevention program.

Immediately dangerous to life and health (IDHL) An atmospheric concentration of any toxic, corrosive, or asphyxiant substance that poses an immediate threat to life or would cause irreversible or delayed adverse health effects or would interfere with an individual's ability to escape from a dangerous atmosphere.

Imminent hazard A complaint alleging that any condition or practice in a workplace is a hazard that could cause death or serious physical harm immediately or before the hazard can be eliminated.

Incident An event, with known causal factors, leading to injury or illness.

Independent adjuster A person who charges a fee to the insurance company to adjust claims.

Independent contractor A fee-for-hire individual who exercises control over how the work is done. Labor law enforcement agencies and the courts look at several factors when deciding if someone is an employee or an independent contractor.

IIPP *See* injury and illness prevention program.

Industrial hygiene A specialized area within the field of occupational health and safety. Industrial hygiene has as its goal the recognition, evaluation, and control of worker exposures to harmful physical or chemical agents or conditions. Industrial hygienists may monitor workplace noise levels, ventilation rates, airborne contaminants, heat exposures, and radiation dose. Various engineering, administrative, and other methods are employed to control or reduce worker exposures.

Industrial safety procedures Specific guidelines for implementing safety regulations and practices in industrial settings. Safety procedures are designed to prevent accidents or acute illnesses, as opposed to many industrial hygiene procedures that reduce chronic

(longer-term) exposures. Examples of safety procedures include those for elevator safety; crane, trench, and construction safety; electrical safety; and confined space safety.

Injuries and Illnesses Log (300) A log, required by federal and state regulations, that documents injuries and illnesses caused by work-related activities that result in lost work time, fatalities, off-site treatment, and restricted work activity. Certain employers are required to maintain and post this information at the worksite posted from February 1 to April 30.

Injury and illness prevention program (IIPP) A health and safety program employers develop and implement.

Inspections Periodic audits of the workplace environment, including equipment, chemicals, building structure, documented procedures, records, and employee knowledge of job requirements and hazards. Inspections may be undertaken for the purpose of departmental self-evaluation or by outside agencies for analysis of compliance with health and safety regulations.

Insurance Institute of America (IIA) Oversees a variety of continuing education programs for professionals in the insurance business and related fields. For example, it oversees the development, testing, and validation for several certifications, such as the Associate of Risk Management (ARM).

Insurer The insurance company that insurer that may provide a workers' compensation policy.

Job Hazard Analysis (JHA) A step-by-step method of identifying the hazards associated with a particular task or job.

Also known as Job Safety Analysis (JSA).

Lanyard A flexible length of rope, wire rope, or strap used to secure the body belt or body harness to a deceleration device, lifeline, or anchorage.

Liability Responsibility to another for one's negligence.

Liability insurance Pays damages to the other party.

Lien (workers' compensation) A right or claim for payment against a worker's compensation case.

Light duty Temporary change in job assignment to accommodate work restrictions.

Litigated claim (workers' compensation) A worker's compensation claim in which an attorney is most likely involved on behalf of the injured worker.

Lockout/block-out (lockout/tagout) Requires that any energy source, whether electrical, hydraulic, mechanical, compressed air, or any other source that might cause unexpected movement, must be disengaged or blocked, and electrical sources must be deenergized and locked or positively sealed in the off position. Even a locked-out machine, however, may not be safe if parts of the machine are not blocked to prevent inadvertent movement. Potential energy that may need to be blocked can come from suspended parts, subject to gravity, or may be energy stored in springs.

Log of Occupational Injuries and Illnesses (OSHA 300) Used by employers to record and classify work-related injuries and illnesses and note the severity. Employers must record in the log information about every work-related death and about every work-related injury or illness that involves loss of consciousness, restricted work activity or job transfer, days away from work, or medical treatment beyond first aid. They must also record significant work-related injuries and illnesses diagnosed by a licensed healthcare professional.

Loss The amount an insurance company pays on a claim.

Loss history Refers to an organization's history of losses (claims). Insurance companies view "loss history" as an indication of an organization's propensity for losses (claims) in the future.

Loss prevention Those activities undertaken to eliminate injuries and illness.

Loss reduction Those activities undertaken to reduce the magnitude or severity of injuries and illnesses.

Machine guarding A cover or other system that prevents objects from getting caught in the moving parts of machinery.

Material-handling equipment Devices like scissor-lifts, pallet jacks, and rolling tables designed to assist in the transport of material.

Material safety data sheets (MSDSs) Literature prepared by a chemical or chemical product manufacturer that contains hazard and safety information about the product. Information typically includes a list of hazardous ingredients, safety precautions for handling, spill or release response procedures, and first-aid instructions.

Medical provider network (MPN) In certain states, an entity or group of healthcare providers set up by an insurer (i.e., a workers' compensation carrier) or self-insured employer to treat workers injured on the job.

Medical treatment Treatment reasonably required to cure or relieve the effects of a work-related injury or illness. Also called medical care.

Mine Safety and Health Administration (MSHA) One of the Department of Labor's specific agencies that oversees surface and subsurface mining safety rules and regulations. MSHA conducts inspections, assists with training and where necessary can issue citations, penalties, and cease-and-desist orders in situations where a mine's safety practices create imminent danger to workers.

Modified work A change in an employee's working conditions in order to accommodate work restrictions.

MPN *See* medical provider network.

MSD *See* musculoskeletal disorder.

MSDS *See* material safety data sheets.

MSHA *See* Mine Safety and Health Administration.

Musculoskeletal disorder (MSD) An injury or illness of soft tissues of the upper extremity (fingers through upper arm), shoulders and neck, low back, and lower extremity (hips through toes) that is primarily caused or exacerbated by workplace risk factors, such as sustained and repeated exertions or awkward postures and manipulations. MSD is a general term denoting muscle, tendon, ligament, nerve, and blood vessel damage caused by work performed in awkward postures or with excessive effort that can result in fatigue, discomfort, and other specific disorders, such as tendonitis or carpal tunnel syndrome.

Musculoskeletal system Includes all the muscles, bones, joints, and cartilage of the body.

National Fire Protection Association (NFPA) A voluntary membership organization whose aim is to promote and improve fire protection and prevention. It publishes 16 volumes of codes known as the National Fire Codes.

National Institute for Occupational Safety and Health (NIOSH) The federal agency responsible for conducting research and making recommendations for the prevention of work-related disease and injury. The institute is part of the Centers for Disease Control and Prevention (CDC).

NFPA *See* National Fire Protection Association.

NIOSH *See* National Institute for Occupational Safety and Health.

Nonrenewal A decision by an insurance company not to renew a policy.

Occupational Safety and Health Administration (OSHA) An agency of the Department of Labor. Its mission is "to save lives, prevent injuries, and protect the health of America's workers."

OSHA *See* Occupational Safety and Health Administration.

Oxygen deficiency That concentration of oxygen by volume below which atmosphere-supplying respiratory protection must be provided. It exists in atmospheres where the percentage of oxygen by volume is less than 19.5% oxygen.

PD *See* permanent disability.

Permanent disability (PD) A legal term (not medical) referring to any lasting disability that results in a reduced earning capacity after maximum medical improvement is reached.

Permanent disability benefits Payments provided when an employee's work injury permanently limits the kinds of work an employee can do.

Personal protective equipment (PPE) Equipment worn or used by workers to protect themselves from exposure to hazardous materials or conditions. The major types of PPE include respirators, eye protection, ear protection, gloves, hard hats, and protective suits.

Physician Depending on the state, may include a medical doctor, osteopath, psychologist, acupuncturist, optometrist, dentist, podiatrist, or chiropractor.

Piece work/piece rate Work that is paid for according to the number of units turned out. A piece rate must be based on an ascertainable figure paid for completing a particular task or making a particular piece of goods.

Policy (insurance) The contract issued by the insurance company to the insured (your business).

Policy period The length of time a policy is in force, from the beginning or effective date to the expiration date.

PPE *See* personal protective equipment.

PPO *See* preferred provider organization.

Preferred Provider Organization (PPO) Hospital, physician, or other provider of healthcare that an insurer recommends to an insured. A PPO allows insurance companies to negotiate directly with hospitals and physicians for health services at a lower price than normally would be charged.

Premium The amount paid by an insured (your business) to an insurance company to obtain or maintain an insurance policy.

Process safety management (PSM) Both a methodology to ensure safety and a set of standards enforced by federal and state OSHA programs. PSM focuses its safety activities on chemical-related systems, such as water treatment plants, chemical manufacturing plants, and similar operations, wherein there are large piping systems, storage, blending, and distribution activities. PSM is specialized in that general industry safety orders do not apply and the magnitude of potential harm to a worker or a community requires significant and specialized planning and safety activities.

PSM *See* process safety management.

Renewal policy A policy issued as a renewal of a policy expiring in the same company.

Repetitive strain injury (RSI) *See* musculoskeletal disorder.

RIMS *See* Risk and Insurance Management Society.

Risk A measure of magnitude or severity if a hazard should manifest.

Risk and Insurance Management Society (RIMS) A national organization that provides ongoing education, training, and information to those in the risk management field. There are dozens of local chapters throughout the United States. The RIMS national conference is a five-day event with speakers as well as exhibits.

RSI Repetitive strain injury; *see* musculoskeletal disorder.

Safety communication The collective means by which safety information is disseminated to employees. Classroom and departmental safety meetings and written communications, such as posters, newsletters, and posting of regulatory agency inspection findings, are included.

Safety coordinators Individuals within departments or colleges who have been appointed by their supervisors or administrators to assist in implementing the workplace safety program in their respective areas.

SARA *See* Superfund Amendments and Reauthorization Act of 1986.

SB198 Historic California Senate Bill (198) requiring employers to adopt and put into place an injury and illness prevention program.

SCBA Self-contained breathing apparatus.

Serious injury or illness One that requires employee hospitalization for more than 24 hours for other than medical observation. Permanent scarring or loss of any part of the body may fall under serious injury.

Serious violation (OSHA) Exists if there is a substantial probability that death or serious physical harm could result from either an exposure that exceeds permissible limits or from practices, methods, operations, or processes used in the workplace.

Social security disability benefits Long-term financial assistance for totally disabled persons. These benefits come from the U.S. Social Security Administration. Benefits may be reduced by workers' compensation payments in some states.

Subjective factors The amount of pain and other symptoms described by an injured worker. Depending on the

state, subjective factors may carry very little weight in comparison to objective measurements.

Subrogation Assignment of rights of recovery from insured.

Supervisors Employees who have authority to direct the tasks of other employees and are therefore responsible for the job-related environments to which their workers are exposed. Where required, supervisors are to develop local area procedures, train their workers regarding health and safety precautions, enforce rules, and maintain records.

Temporary disability benefits Payments paid when an employee loses wages because of an injury that prevents her from her usual job while recovering.

Terrorism The use of force to demoralize, intimidate, and subjugate. A political weapon or policy.

Third-party administrator (TPA) An organization that performs managerial and clerical functions related to an employee benefit insurance plan or insurance plan, such as workers' compensation.

Threat An indication of imminent danger or a source of harm.

Title 29 The section of the Code of Federal Regulations dealing with the regulations of the Occupational Safety and Health Administration.

Toeboards Provided on all open sides and ends of railed scaffolds at locations where people work or pass under the scaffold and at all interior floor, roof, and shaft openings. A standard toeboard is four inches minimum from its top edge to the level of the floor, platform, runway, or ramp and must be securely fastened in place. It may be made of any substantial material, either solid or with openings not over one inch in greatest dimension.

Toolbox or tailgate safety meetings Short (10- to 15-minute) on-the-job meetings in construction and heavy industry held to keep employees apprised of work-related hazards. In most states these should be conducted every 10 days.

TPA *See* third-party administrator.

Training Classroom instruction, job-site safety meetings, on-the-job training, and written materials provided to employees to make them aware of workplace hazards and how to prevent accidents and illnesses.

Underwriter The person who reviews an application for insurance and decides if your company is acceptable and what premium to charge.

Underwriting The process an insurance company uses to decide whether to accept or reject an application for a policy.

Universal precautions An approach to infection control. According to the concept of universal precautions, all human blood and certain human body fluids are treated as if known to be infectious for HIV, the hepatitis B and C viruses, and other bloodborne pathogens.

UR *See* utilization review.

Utilization review (UR) The process insurance companies use to decide whether to authorize and pay for treatment.

Willful violation Occurs when the employer commits an intentional and knowing violation of safety law or when the employer did not consciously violate a safety law but was aware that an unsafe or hazardous condition existed and made no reasonable effort to eliminate the condition.

WMSD Work-related musculoskeletal disorder. *Also see* musculoskeletal disorder.

Workplace safety program A program that aims to develop a long-term plan that is successful in protecting people from injury and death, that complies with regulations, and controls the associated financial costs of loss. Such programs encompass many technical disciplines.

Work restrictions Typically a doctor's description of the work an employee can and cannot do.

Index